RUSSIA RISING

RUSSIA RISING

TRACKING THE BEAR IN BIBLE PROPHECY

MARK HITCHCOCK

TYNDALE
MOMENTUM™

The nonfiction imprint of
Tyndale House Publishers, Inc.

Library of Congress Cataloging-in-Publication Data
Names: Hitchcock, Mark, date, author.
Title: Russia rising : tracking the bear in Bible prophecy / Mark Hitchcock.
Description: Carol Stream, Illinois : Tyndale House Publishers, Inc., 2017. | Includes bibliographical references.
Identifiers: LCCN 2017027217| ISBN 9781496429650 (hc) | ISBN 9781496428073 (sc)
Subjects: LCSH: Bible—Prophecies—Former Soviet republics.
Classification: LCC BS649.R9 H588 2017 | DDC 220.1/5—dc23 LC record available at https://lccn.loc.gov/2017027217

Printed in the United States of America

23	22	21	20	19	18	17
7	6	5	4	3	2	1

To my first granddaughter, Cameron Joy Hitchcock, who brings unspeakable joy to my life and to our entire family. May our gracious God bless you and keep you all the days of your life.

Contents

CHAPTER 1

THERE IS A BEAR IN THE WOODS

A BEAR WILL NOT ASK ANYONE FOR PERMISSION.

VLADIMIR PUTIN

During the 1984 presidential campaign, candidate Ronald Reagan used a television commercial that's become known for its compelling opening line—"There is a bear in the woods."

The ad featured a grizzly bear wandering menacingly through a forest while the narrator said, "There is a bear in the woods. For some people, the bear is easy to see. Others don't see it at all. Some people say the bear is tame. Others say it's vicious and dangerous. Since no one can really be sure who's right, isn't it smart to be as strong as the bear? If there is a bear."

A man appears in the closing scene, and the bear takes

a step back. The captivating ad concludes with a picture of Reagan and the tagline "President Reagan: Prepared for Peace." Reagan took the Bear seriously, and in December 1991, the Soviet Union collapsed, no longer dominating Eastern Europe.

Fast-forward almost thirty years, and no one doubts there's a bear in the woods. Russia is back. The Russian bear has roared out of hibernation and into the headlines. The Bear is back—but what does that mean for our world?

The movie *The Revenant* depicts one of the most savage, vicious scenes in cinematic annals. Not far into the movie, frontiersman and fur trapper Hugh Glass (played by Leonardo DiCaprio) unwittingly gets between a mother grizzly bear and her cubs. Without warning, he's slammed to the ground by the charging grizzly. It happens so quickly he doesn't have time even to turn and raise his rifle. The ferocious mauling is so brutal and unrelenting, it's difficult to watch. Glass's broken, lacerated body is left near death. The lesson is clear: get between a mother grizzly and her cubs, and the result won't be pretty.

BACK TO THE USSR

Since 1991 and the collapse of the Soviet Union, Vladimir Putin and others of his ilk have felt like a mother bear robbed of her cubs, willing to maul anyone who stands in the way of restoring Soviet greatness. Putin, a former KGB lieutenant colonel, became Russian prime minister in August 1999 and president in May 2000. He was reelected in 2004, then bowed out for his pupil Dmitry Medvedev to assume the presidency. But Putin ran successfully again in 2012. There's no sign now that he will ever step down again. *Forbes* ranked Putin as the world's most powerful person for the fourth year in a row in 2016.[1]

During his 2005 State of the Nation address to parliament, Putin lamented that the demise of the Soviet Union was "the greatest geopolitical catastrophe" of the century.[2] Ukrainian foreign minister Pavlo Klimkin wrote in the *Guardian*, "Reversing the breakup of the Soviet Union and restoring the Russian empire have now become an obsession for the Kremlin."[3]

The obsession has gone so far that the Kremlin is commissioning new statues of Joseph Stalin, one of the twentieth century's worst mass murderers.[4] This is certainly a chilling window into the current Russian psyche.

Putin seizes every opportunity to stoke smoldering resentment within Russia and to draw attention to the perceived threats against his nation in order to take more and more aggressive actions to reestablish the empire. With every passing day, the Bear gets more bellicose. Putin has launched a crusade to rebuild the empire that fell along with the Berlin Wall.

President Obama promised a Russian reset in 2009 when he took office, but the opposite has occurred. US-Russian relations have relapsed into a Cold War 2.0, and some say the current situation is even worse than the Cold War. Slowly and subtly Europe and the West have sleepwalked into a new era of danger and instability. In just a little more than a decade, "the unthinkable has become a reality. Russia, seemingly finished after its defeat in the Cold War, now is emerging as a prospective great power challenging the West."[5]

Russia is on the march. General Sir Richard Shirreff, the former Deputy Supreme Allied Commander of NATO, said of Vladimir Putin, "[he] is calling the shots at the moment."[6]

That the Russian bear is on the prowl is clearly evidenced by the steady stream of world headlines:

"Russia's Rising Empire"

NATIONAL REVIEW, AUGUST 9, 2016

"The Russian Bear Is Rising"

HUFFINGTON POST, SEPTEMBER 2, 2016

"Beware: The Russian Bear Is Getting Bolder"

WASHINGTON POST, DECEMBER 1, 2016

"Russia's Rising Role in the World"

FOREIGN POLICY NEWS, DECEMBER 30, 2016

Russian aggression has moved into a new phase that threatens international order and stability. General James Mattis, the US defense secretary, has called Russia the world's top threat, and Senator John McCain agrees, calling Vladimir Putin "the premier and most important threat, more so than ISIS.[7] In all the Bear's bluster, we sometimes forget that Russia possesses the world's largest stockpile of nuclear weapons, with more than seven thousand nuclear warheads.[8]

Putin's grand goals are to destroy the West by breaking up the European Union, dividing NATO, frustrating and unnerving the United States, and expanding Russia's global influence. On all fronts Russia seems to be succeeding.

The Bear is on the move, leaving its footprints across the globe. First, it was Georgia in 2008. Next, the Bear invaded and annexed Crimea in 2014 and supported separatists in eastern Ukraine. In 2015, Russia, working in tandem with Iran, sent armed forces and especially air power into Syria to prop up Bashar al-Assad's crumbling regime. We're facing a new "Red Dawn." Russia is pulling the strings in the Middle East. Putin is trying to break NATO. He yearns to bring Eastern Europe and the Baltic States back into the Russian orbit.

Despite that Russia is the world's largest nation,[9] the Bear is hungry for more. Putin is busily canvassing the globe in search of weak prey and willing allies. And he's finding no shortage on either front. The Kremlin, with assistance from Iran, is arming the Taliban in Afghanistan. There are reports of Russian activity in Nicaragua. Putin's territory grab extends even to the Arctic Circle, which holds more than one-quarter of the world's undiscovered oil and gas. He visited the area in 2017, and plans are under way to construct a massive military base there. The top of the world is a top Russian priority.

FANCY BEAR AND COZY BEAR

While many Americans may not be fully aware of all that Russia is doing around the world, Russia has dominated US headlines in 2017 because of its meddling in the 2016 US presidential election. By now everyone is well aware Russia has perfected cyber-terrorism and cyber-espionage. Global technological dependence has been weaponized.

The computer-hacking scheme and interference in the US elections has been directly tied to Russian spy agencies and was part of a larger strategy that included hacking computers of the Democratic National Committee. Nearly twenty thousand e-mails hacked by the Russians were dumped by WikiLeaks on July 22, 2016—just three days before the Democratic National Convention—and embarrassed many Democratic Party leaders.

The cyber-security firm CrowdStrike gave these Russian cyber-criminals names—"Fancy Bear" and "Cozy Bear":

> Traditionally, Cozy Bear targets potential victims
> with phishing attacks—email messages that appear
> to be from a legitimate, trusted friend or associate.
> Those messages may contain malicious software
> that scans a machine for antivirus software, then
> plants malware on the target machine that make
> it possible for attackers to monitor keystrokes,
> communications, documents and other sensitive
> material on target computers. Fancy Bear is known

for stealing targets' usernames and passwords by setting up dummy websites that appear real enough to convince users to input their email and password information.[10]

Russian attempts to influence American politics are nothing new. In the 1960s "Soviet intelligence officers spread a rumor that the U.S. government was involved in the assassination of Martin Luther King, Jr." In the 1980s "they spread the rumor that American intelligence had 'created' the AIDS virus, at Fort Detrick, Maryland. They regularly lent support to leftist parties and insurgencies."[11] Russian intelligence services have been sifting through computer networks in the United States for more than a decade.

One of Russia's strategies is known as *dezinformatsiya*, "false information intended to discredit the official version of events, or the very notion of reliable truth."[12] We know this strategy better today as "fake news." Due to the increasing polarization in the American political landscape and the fractured media environment, Russia views the United States as a ripe target for this tactic.

Former Director of National Intelligence James Clapper testified before the Senate regarding "an unprecedented Russian effort to interfere in the U.S. electoral process. The operation involved hacking Democrats' e-mails, publicizing the stolen contents through WikiLeaks, and manipulating social media to spread 'fake news.'"[13] The e-mail hacks are part of a much larger strategy to damage American confidence and undermine Western power and alliances. Again, Russia's meddling in other nations' elections is nothing new. Just ask the Europeans. Russia's "Red Web," as its espionage efforts have been called, has worked to exert influence on German and French elections as well.

The best term to describe Russia's strategy, according to historian Angus E. Goldberg, "is the Russian word 'bespredel,' which means 'absence of limits,' or 'anything goes.'"[14] What we see today is "bespredel" on steroids—a dangerous new game of Russian roulette.

Russian meddling in US elections combined with Russia's growing international aggression has pushed US-Russian relations to a troubling low point. Sergey Rogov, academic director of the Institute for US and Canadian Studies in Moscow, says that hostility between the United States and Russia is deeper than it has been in years. He adds, "I spent many years in the trenches of the first Cold War, and I don't want to die in the trenches of the second. We are back to 1983. . . . It's frightening."[15] The world has descended into a Putin-led Cold War 2.0. Consider these current headlines:

"Trump, Putin, and the New Cold War"

NEW YORKER, MARCH 6, 2017

"Cold War 2.0?"

MSNBC, SEPTEMBER 29, 2016

"Vladimir Putin's Outlaw State"

NEW YORK TIMES, SEPTEMBER 29, 2016

"Russian Hacking and the 2016 Election"

CNN, DECEMBER 16, 2016

In addition to its cyber-espionage, Russia is constantly testing US patience and resolve with pinprick provocations. Russian bombers are flying off the coast of Alaska. Russian spy ships are loitering off the east coast of the United States. Russia's acts appear to be carefully calculated and measured. Putin doesn't want to cross the line and spark open confrontation with the United States, but he knows that micro-aggressions will be tolerated—to a point. Russia may also be testing the waters to see how far its intimidations can go without incurring a response from the US, or these may just be Putin's attempts to constantly remind the world that Russia is relevant again. Whatever the Russian motivation for these actions may be, one thing is clear: the Bear is working on all fronts to let the US and the world know that there is a bear in the woods.

DESERT BEAR

As the Kremlin is combing the world for soft spots to exert its influence, the Middle East and North Africa are key targets. Putin is taking advantage of the unrest, instability, and chaos in these places to promote his expansionist agenda. The disarray in the Middle East and North Africa has proved to be fertile soil for Putin's unbridled ambition to bring back the Russian empire. Russia is working to bring Libya, Sudan, Turkey, and Iran under its umbrella. But the linchpin in Russia's push into the Middle East is Syria, where the Kremlin has thrown in with the devil, supporting the diabolical tyrant Bashar al-Assad. Russian troops and aircraft poured into Syria in 2015. Russian air power combined with Iranian ground support is propping up the Assad regime. Russia is entrenched in Syria, even establishing a naval port in Tartus, giving Russia the warm-water port it has coveted.

The United States is already engaged in a proxy war with Russia in Syria that's been going on for several years with both powers supporting different sides in the Syrian civil war. After the US Tomahawk missile strike of a Syrian air base on April 6, 2017, Russia and Iran warned the US of crossing "red lines" and raised the prospect of war. Without a doubt, Syria is a dangerous flash point. With Russian and Iranian troops stationed there and the United States launching missile strikes, the potential for a serious misstep is ever present. Any wrong move there could push the world to the brink of disaster. The Russian-Iranian alliance in Syria has put troops from these two nations ominously on Israel's northern border. Russia's new allies would love nothing more than to drive the Jewish state into the sea.

All of this forces us to reckon with some serious questions. Is what we're witnessing just geopolitical coincidence, or could there be a hidden hand behind it all? Is it possible that the rise of Russia and the alliances that the Bear is forming are part of something bigger? Could it be the buildup for the fulfillment of ancient prophecies from Scripture? Is this another prophetic signpost that the world is racing toward the end of days?

CODE RED

On January 26, 2017, the Science and Security Board for the *Bulletin of the Atomic Scientists* moved the minute hand on the Doomsday Clock ahead thirty seconds, bringing it to two minutes and thirty seconds to midnight. This is "the closest the clock has been to midnight since 1953."[16] Among the reasons for the move were the rise of nationalism and the possibility of a renewed arms race between the United States and Russia.

People everywhere seem to sense that world events are moving toward an apocalyptic showdown. According to a recent poll, "41% of all U.S. adults, 54% of Protestants and 77% of Evangelicals believe the world is now living in the biblical end times."[17]

A Pew Research poll found that

- 72 percent of Americans expect the world to face a major world energy crisis,
- 58 percent think it "definite or probable" that there will be another world war, and
- 41 percent believe Jesus Christ will return by the year 2050.[18]

Additionally, a 2004 *Time*/CNN poll found that 59 percent of Americans believe the prophecies of the book of Revelation will come to pass.[19] Similar polls have revealed the following:

- 55 percent of Americans believe "that before the world ends the religiously faithful will be saved."
- 46 percent of Americans agree with this statement: "The world will end in the Battle of Armageddon between Jesus and the Antichrist."[20]

Similarly, "research conducted by the Brookings Institute's Center for Middle East Policy on Americans' attitudes toward the Middle East and Israel found that 79 percent of Evangelicals say they believe 'that the unfolding violence across the Middle East is a sign that the end times are nearer.'"[21]

Concerning the terrible civil war in Syria, "almost one in three Americans see Syria's recent conflict as part of the Bible's plan for the end times. One in four thinks that a U.S. military strike in Syria could lead to Armageddon. One in five believes the world will end in their lifetime."[22]

These statistics reveal that people everywhere have serious questions—searching questions—about how recent events, including the rise of Russia, relate to the ancient prophecies of the Bible.

And the Bible is certainly the best place to look for answers. The Bible is a book of prophecy. Almost 30 percent of the Bible was prophecy at the time it was written. Scripture contains about one thousand prophecies, and about five hundred of them have been literally fulfilled with 100 percent accuracy. That's quite a track record, setting the Bible far apart from any other holy book. Unlike the predictions of astrologers, mystics, and mediums, the prophecies of the Bible aren't vague and general predictions that can be altered to accommodate any situation. The prophecies recorded in the Bible are detailed and intricately interwoven. The specificity of the Bible's prophecies and its stellar track record continue to draw people to its pages for insight into the future. Even the most skeptical person can put the prophecies of Scripture to the test. In light of current events, prophecies formerly brushed aside as incredible or speculative are now being carefully examined again.

We must never forget that while the prophecies of the Bible never change, world events are constantly in flux. The Bible, not cable news, is our prophetic plumb line, the standard by which we measure everything else. Nevertheless, today's headlines are increasingly aligning with ancient biblical prophecies that describe an end-times scenario not unlike what we see today.

FUTURE SHOCK

The Jewish prophet Ezekiel, writing more than 2,500 years ago, foretold a Russian-led invasion of Israel in the end times. Russia's allies in this predicted offensive are a group of Islamic nations that are forming closer ties with the Bear as you're reading these words. Russia is rising right on schedule and is expanding its influence in the Middle East just as the Bible predicts. That's precisely what we should expect if the coming of Christ is drawing near.

When we track the Bear in biblical prophecy, we discover its footprints lead to the Middle East—and ultimately to the land of Israel. Israel is ground zero for the events of the end times.

But why Israel? As David Jeremiah comments, "Israel is one of the smallest nations on earth. It is one-nineteenth the size of California and roughly the size of New Jersey. Russia is 785 times larger than Israel. Israel measures approximately 290 miles at its longest, 85 miles at its widest, and 9 miles at its narrowest."[23] Charles Dyer and Mark Tobey offer some explanation:

> From a human perspective Israel ought to occupy nothing more than a minor supporting part in any worldwide drama. In terms of geographical size, Israel ranks 148th among the nations of the world, nestled between Belize and El Salvador. Her standing improves slightly when ranked by population. At just over eight million, Israel breaks the top 100, coming in 98th between Switzerland and Honduras. And when comparing gross domestic product (GDP), Israel is ranked between 34th and 37th, depending on which organization is doing the measuring. Still, that puts Israel in with countries such as Malaysia,

Singapore, and Hong Kong with barely one-quarter
the GDP of a country like Mexico.

God, however, uses a different standard of
measurement. And in His eyes Israel ranks at the top
of the list in terms of national significance.[24]

God made unconditional promises to the descendants
of Abraham, Isaac, and Jacob that have not been fulfilled—
promises involving the land of Israel. But before these promises are fulfilled, Scripture tells us that the people of Israel must
go through a time of trouble and tribulation that will turn
them to the Lord. Consistent with these ancient prophecies,
the modern state of Israel exists, is under constant pressure
by the international community, and is surrounded by a sea
of enemies who will play a role in the tribulation Israel will
endure. The tiny nation of Israel is at the center of world attention, just as we should expect if the end of the age is drawing
near. At the same time, Russia is the new power broker in the
Middle East. The convergence of these events and many more
that we see in the headlines every day strikingly foreshadows
the ancient prophecy of Ezekiel 38–39. What we see today in
light of this passage in Ezekiel raises many questions:

- Is the rise of Russia in the end times *really* predicted in
  the Bible, or is this just "headline theology"?
- Who are Russia's end-times allies?
- Does the Bible say anything about Russia's ties with
  Iran?

- What events will precipitate the Russian invasion of Israel?
- Will Israel survive?
- How soon could the Bear make its final push to the south?
- Does the United States play any role in these events?
- What does it all mean?

We'll answer these questions, and many more, as we track the Bear through the pages of Bible prophecy. Our spiritual GPS for tracking the Bear is primarily found in the ancient prophecies of Ezekiel 38–39. You will find these chapters at the end of this book in appendix 1 (page 163). I recommend that you read these chapters from God's inspired Word now to prepare you for the rest of this book.

I, and many others, believe Russia's rising in current events reveals a trajectory that points toward the ultimate fulfillment of Ezekiel's prophecy . . . maybe very soon!

CHAPTER 2

THE FINAL GAME OF THRONES

IT ALL LOOKS AS IF THE WORLD IS PREPARING FOR WAR.
MIKHAIL GORBACHEV IN *TIME* MAGAZINE (2017)

WHEN YOU PLAY A GAME OF THRONES YOU WIN OR YOU DIE.
GEORGE R. R. MARTIN, *A GAME OF THRONES*

Just days before his crucifixion, Jesus led his disciples from the Temple down through the Kidron Valley and up the Mount of Olives, which overlooks the Temple precincts. From that vantage point he pulled back the prophetic curtain and laid out a stunning, yet simple, blueprint for the end of days. This sermon, known as the Olivet discourse, begins with a list of signs that will portend his return to earth. Jesus likened these events to birth pains that will intensify in severity and get closer and closer together:

> Don't let anyone mislead you, for many will come in my name, claiming, "I am the Messiah." They will

deceive many. And you will hear of wars and threats of wars, but don't panic. Yes, these things must take place, but the end won't follow immediately. Nation will go to war against nation, and kingdom against kingdom. There will be famines and earthquakes in many parts of the world. But all this is only the first of the birth pains, with more to come.

MATTHEW 24:4-8

After talking about false messiahs, Jesus mentions the second birth pain: "wars and threats of wars" and "nation [going] to war against nation, and kingdom against kingdom." This prophecy is mirrored by the apostle John in Revelation 6:3-4, which predicts the outbreak of wars during the end times using the symbol of a rider with a sword on a blood-red horse. The fragile, relative sense of peace the world experiences today will be shattered and suddenly stripped from the earth (see 1 Thessalonians 5:1-3).

While "wars and threats of wars" have always been part of human history, international strife and conflict will mushroom and proliferate in the end times to levels never seen before. I think we can sense the foreshocks of that today. Peace is tentative. Threats of wars are rumbling. The Middle East is like a powder keg ready to explode—fueled by ISIS, Syria, Iran, the Israeli-Palestinian standoff, Hezbollah, Hamas, and Al-Qaeda. Some small yet reckless act could unleash total chaos.

Bad actors all over the world seem ready to spin out of

control at any time. North Korea and its loony leader are conducting ballistic and nuclear weapons tests. The Russian bear is on the prowl all over the globe. Other hot spots could ignite suddenly. The winds of war are blowing.

How much longer can this all be kept in check?

How much longer until the lid blows off?

THE FINAL FOUR

In the strife between nations and kingdoms that will crest during the end times, the Bible highlights four "kings" or leaders who will ascend to power. While the world of the last days will be engulfed with "wars and threats of wars . . . nation . . . against nation, and kingdom against kingdom," four key leaders will emerge from the pack, locking themselves and their allies in a final, deadly game of thrones. Scripture speaks of this final game of thrones as nations and kingdoms jockeying for power and preeminence. In the end times, four kings will take center stage in a dramatic geopolitical death struggle.

These leaders and their power blocs will rise and fall at different times. This book is primarily about the rise of Russia—which, as we'll see, the Bible identifies as the king of the north. We don't want to get too far ahead of ourselves, but for us to understand the rise of Russia and the northern confederacy, it's helpful to get an overview of the end-times alignments of nations.

In the scramble for power and resources, the world will divide into four main power blocs:

- The king of the west (see Daniel 7:8; Revelation 13:1-10)
- The king of the south (see Daniel 11:40)
- The king of the north (see Ezekiel 38; Daniel 11:40)
- The kings of the east (see Revelation 16:12)

The directional location of each of these powers is given in relation to Israel, which from God's perspective is the center, or "navel," of the earth (see Ezekiel 38:12, NASB). Pointing to these four power blocs of the end times, Bible prophecy scholar J. Dwight Pentecost says,

> In studying the alignments of Gentile nations at the time of the tribulation period we find there will be: (1) a ten kingdom federation of nations that has become the final form of the fourth kingdom or the Roman empire under the leadership of the Beast [Antichrist] (Rev. 13:1-10); (2) a northern confederacy, Russia and her allies; (3) an eastern or Asiatic confederacy; and (4) a north African power. The movements of these four allied powers against Palestine [Israel] in the tribulation period are clearly stated in Scripture and constitute one of the major themes of prophecy.[1]

The two main objectives of these four kings will be the same—dominate the world and destroy Israel. The common goals they seek will pit them against one another. The ultimate prize in this final game of thrones is the tiny land of Israel, which means all of this was set in motion by the rebirth of the modern state of Israel in 1948, as predicted in Ezekiel 37. The stage is being set for the rise of these kings.

Of course, the Bible doesn't mention every nation on earth in the end times, so we can't be sure exactly which nations will be part of these blocs. Also, it's impossible to say that all nations will be part of one of these coalitions. But when the dust settles, these four will be key players according to Scripture.

The King of the West

The first king who will appear on the world scene is a leader often called the "king of the west," although the Bible never gives him that designation. This title is fitting, however, because he will lead the reconstituted, revived, and reunited Roman empire or Western alliance of nations. The world knows him best as the Antichrist.

Daniel 2 and 7 reveal that a group of ten Western leaders will come to power sometime after the church is raptured to heaven. These ten leaders will serve as a kind of ruling committee or oligarchy over the Western confederacy of nations. In Daniel 2 they're represented by the ten toes on the metallic image, while in Daniel 7 they're pictured by ten horns on the fourth beast. They represent the final form of the Roman empire. I like to call them the "Group of Ten" or "G-10." The European Union could be an embryonic form of this final alignment of nations or simply the first stage of some greater alliance of nations. Either way, the Bible is clear that when the end times arrive, these ten kings or leaders will have control over the Western nations.

At some point, one ruler—the final Antichrist—will emerge, and he will grab control over the reunited Roman empire. He is depicted by Daniel as a "small horn" that rises up among the ten horns (Daniel 7:8). With the rule of this leader, the revived Roman empire will mimic the historical Roman empire that transitioned from a republic to an empire—from the rule of a body of leaders to rule by one caesar. As the Antichrist seizes control of the Western federation, the Bible says he will consolidate and expand his power, ultimately ruling the entire world for the final three and a half years before the return of Christ.

The Western leader is the subject of more than one hundred Bible passages. The Bible paints a vivid portrait of this end-times dictator:

- He will be a Gentile, not a Jew (see Revelation 13:1).[2]
- He will burst onto the world scene as a peacemaker, forging a seven-year agreement or peace treaty with Israel, solving (albeit temporarily) the Middle East crisis (see Daniel 9:27; Revelation 6:1-2).[3]
- He will break the seven-year treaty at its midpoint, double-crossing the Jewish people (see Daniel 9:27). At this point, his mask of moderation will come off.
- As the final great anti-Semite, he will unleash a reign of terror against the Jewish people (see Daniel 7:25).
- He will declare himself to be God and will demand

worship (see Daniel 11:37; 2 Thessalonians 2:4; Revelation 13:4, 12).[4]

- He will defile the rebuilt Jewish Temple in Jerusalem by establishing an image of himself in the Holy of Holies (see Matthew 24:15; 2 Thessalonians 2:4).
- He will have a lieutenant and propaganda minister known as the "false prophet" (see Revelation 13:11-15; 16:13-14; 19:20).
- He will force people to bear his "mark" to participate in the world economic system he establishes (see Revelation 13:16-18). He will control the one-world economic system of the end times.

The final king of the west is identified in Scripture by many different names and titles that shed light on his character and career:

- The small horn (see Daniel 7:8)
- A king, insolent and skilled in intrigue (see Daniel 8:23)
- The prince who is to come (see Daniel 9:26)
- The one who makes desolate (see Daniel 9:27)
- The king who does as he pleases (see Daniel 11:36-45)
- The man of destruction (see 2 Thessalonians 2:3)
- The man of lawlessness (see 2 Thessalonians 2:8)
- The Antichrist (see 1 John 2:18)
- The rider on the white horse (see Revelation 6:2)
- The beast out of the sea (see Revelation 13:1-2)

The Western king will be nothing short of a satanic masterpiece—a satanic superman.

Human history begins with the sin of man and ends with the man of sin.

The King of the South

Another end-times king will rise from North Africa, probably Egypt, and he is called the king of the south (see Daniel 11:40). Daniel 11:1-35a discusses the past kings of the south who ruled Egypt, but in Daniel 11:35b, the text jumps from the past to the future—from history to prophecy. The leap to the end times is signaled by the words, "until the time of the end, for the appointed time is still to come." Daniel 11:40 also places these verses in an end-times setting—"at the time of the end."

J. Dwight Pentecost identifies this last-days leader: "Evidently this King of the South is allied with the King of the North, for they simultaneously invade Palestine (Dan. 11:40). There is general agreement among interpreters that the King of the South has reference to Egypt, inasmuch as Egypt is frequently referred to as the land to the south in Scripture."[5] This alliance will probably include other nations from the area such as Libya and Sudan, referenced in Ezekiel 38, and possibly Algeria and Tunisia.

A North African alliance will be part of the end-times scenario. The king of the south will be in league with the king of the north. We will look at this alliance more in depth in chapter 4.

The King of the North

Russia is identified as the king of the north in Daniel 11:40 and is further described in Ezekiel 38–39. Daniel 11:5-35 describes the back-and-forth struggle between Egypt (the king of the south) and the ancient Seleucid empire centered in Syria (the king of the north). Israel was caught between these two ancient powers for centuries.

Daniel 11:40 refers to a king of the north who will rise in the end times. This leader, like the ancient Seleucids, will control a vast swath of territory north and east of Israel. The prophetic counterpart to the historical Seleucid monarchs is Russia. Russia's identification as the king of the north is confirmed by the parallel passage in Ezekiel 38, which describes a northern alliance that invades Israel in the end times.

We'll discuss Russia's role much more in the pages to come, but there's one final human king who's part of the end-times game of thrones.

The Kings of the East

This is the only one of the four power blocs whose leader's title is plural—"kings," not "king." The kings of the east are specifically referenced just one time in Scripture. Revelation 16:12 says, "Then the sixth angel poured out his bowl on the great Euphrates River, and it dried up so that the kings from the east could march their armies toward the west without hindrance."

The specific nations in this coalition are not listed. All we know is that they come from east of the Euphrates River, since the river must be dried up for their march into the land of Israel.

John Walvoord notes,

> The most simple and suitable explanation is to take the passage literally. The Euphrates River then becomes the geographic boundary of the ancient Roman Empire. The kings of the east are kings from the east or "of the sunrising," that is, monarchs who originated in the Orient. . . . If the drying of the Euphrates River is to be taken literally, then what can be understood by the reference to "the kings of the east"? Here again the literal view is to be preferred. Inasmuch as it would be most natural in a world war culminating in the Middle East to have the Orient represented, the interpretation that views the kings of the east as the political and military leaders of Asiatic forces east of the Euphrates is a satisfactory solution.[6]

Revelation 16:14 reveals that the movement of the kings of the east into Israel is part of a worldwide gathering of the "rulers of the world . . . for battle against the Lord on that great judgment day of God the Almighty." According to Revelation 16:16, the geographical focal point of the gathering is Armageddon (Mount Megiddo in northern Israel).

This army from the east in Revelation 16 is often connected with the army of 200 million in Revelation 9:16. Some take a further step and associate this massive army with China. If this view is correct, it's astounding, because when the apostle John wrote these words, 200 million would have been close to the population of the entire world. My view is that the army of 200 million in Revelation is a demonic horde that will come forth in the end times.[7]

Either way, a great army from east of the Euphrates will be a key part of the wars of the end times.

PUTTING THE PIECES TOGETHER

I hate puzzles and am terrible at assembling them, but early on I discovered a very simple guideline—the key to putting together a puzzle is the picture on top of the box. The assembled pieces must look like the picture. I also learned that you have to begin with the edge pieces to frame the picture. What's true of putting together a cardboard puzzle is also true of putting together the prophetic picture in Scripture. As we look at our world today, the picture we see is steadily looking more and more like the picture we see in the Bible. The edges seem to be taking form, and some of the picture is beginning to fill in. The rise of the four kings is part of the picture.

THE FINAL FOUR KINGS	
The king of the west	Western powers under the rule of the Antichrist; the reunited Roman empire
The king of the south	North African coalition
The kings of the east	Grouping of nations from east of the Euphrates River
The king of the north	Russian-led alliance

Today, many key Western nations are allied in the agreements of NATO. The European Union is a further cementing of Western interests. Radical Islam has ignited the Muslim nations of North Africa, and we can see how they could form into a southern coalition. Russia is emerging and establishing alliances with other nations north and east of Israel. To the east of the Euphrates River are a host of nations that could coalesce into the predicted kings of the east. Certainly, many twists and turns will occur in the days ahead, reshaping and reforming current headlines, but the edges of the puzzle appear to be taking shape.

Putting this final game of thrones together, we see that sometime after the rapture of all believers in Christ to heaven, the first move is made by the king of the west, who will begin the seven-year Tribulation by forging some kind of peace agreement or treaty with Israel. At some point, the kings of the north (Russia and its Islamic allies) and south (likely Egypt and the nations of North Africa) will invade Israel. Their attack will have two objectives: 1) wiping out the Jewish people and stealing their land, and 2) challenging the authority of the Western king (who has a treaty with Israel). Charles Ryrie describes their attack on Israel as a pincer move: "A pincer is an instrument with two claws used to grab something. . . . The King of the South is situated perfectly: right on the southern doorstep of the land that is up for grabs. Russia will form the northern claw, Egypt the southern claw; put them together . . . and you have the pincer. The attack will be launched on both fronts simultaneously."[8]

After the kings of the north and south are destroyed by God, the king of the west (the Antichrist) will surge to global ascendancy. Finally, at the end of the seven-year Great Tribulation, the kings of the east will make their move as they cross the Euphrates River and pour into the land of Israel along with the remainder of the armies from around the world. The armies will muster at Armageddon in northern Israel. With the kings of the east and the Antichrist gathered in the land, there's one final King who will make his move.

THE FIFTH KING

To make sure we have the full story, the final move in the end-times game of thrones is the return of the King of kings to take back planet Earth. His move will occur at Armageddon when he crushes the forces of the king of the west and the kings of the east, as well as the remaining armies from around the globe. Recently, the United States dropped a bomb on ISIS in Afghanistan called MOAB (the mother of all bombs). Revelation 19 describes the final MOAB—the mother of all battles. Revelation 19:11-21 describes the King who comes to take his rightful throne in a righteous bloodbath. The second coming of Christ will be as different as one can imagine from his first coming as a baby in Bethlehem.

There's an often-told story that Vernon Grounds relates. When a friend of Grounds's was in seminary, he would play basketball at a public school because there was no gym at the seminary. Each week as he and some other seminarians played, an elderly janitor would wait patiently until they were finished. He always sat in the stands reading his Bible. One day Grounds's friend approached the custodian. "What are you reading?" he asked. The janitor answered, "The book of Revelation." Grounds's friend was surprised. "Do you understand what you're reading?" "Oh, yes," the janitor replied. The seminarian was even more surprised and asked, "What does it mean?" The janitor answered him, "It means that Jesus is gonna win." Grounds writes, "That's the best commentary I have ever heard on that book. Jesus is going to win."[9]

Jesus wins the final game of thrones. None can stand against him. All will wither under his mighty hand.

It's great to get the big picture in mind and know up front who the key players are and how the story ends. But we've gotten way ahead of ourselves. Now that we have a broad overview of some of the events of the end times, we're going to slow down, back up a bit, and look in detail at key prophecies that must be fulfilled before Jesus comes, including the rise and fall of Russia.

Let's zero in on the king of the north and track the Bear in Bible prophecy.

CHAPTER 3

IS RUSSIA REALLY IN THE BIBLE?

EZEKIEL SAYS THAT . . . THE NATION THAT WILL LEAD ALL THE OTHER POWERS
INTO DARKNESS AGAINST ISRAEL WILL COME OUT OF THE NORTH. WHAT OTHER
POWERFUL NATION IS TO THE NORTH OF ISRAEL [BESIDES RUSSIA]? NONE.

RONALD REAGAN[1]

Ezekiel 38 is the biblical entry point for any discussion of
Russia in biblical prophecy. All agree the names *Russia* and
Moscow do not appear in this chapter or anywhere else in the
Bible. Yet as you will see, many reputable scholars believe that
the ancient prophet refers to the nation we know today as
Russia. Ezekiel 38:1-2 is the beginning of a list of nations that
will join together, forming a northern storm in the end times:
"The word of the LORD came to me saying, 'Son of man, set
your face toward Gog of the land of Magog, the prince of
Rosh, Meshech and Tubal, and prophesy against him'" (NASB).

Two key words in this verse have been associated with
Russia—*Rosh* and *Magog*. Some claim that any attempt to

associate these ancient places with modern Russia is speculative and sensationalistic.[2] Others believe the ancient prophet
identified the ruler of the modern nation of Russia as the final
king of the north described in Daniel 11:40. To discover which
view carries more weight, we have to examine the evidence.
But before we look at Ezekiel 38, let's briefly consider one
other biblical passage that some have associated with Russia.

THE RISING BEAR IN DANIEL 7

Because of the symbolism of a bear, some believe Daniel 7:5
is a reference to modern Russia: "Then I saw a second beast,
and it looked like a bear. It was rearing up on one side, and it
had three ribs in its mouth between its teeth. And I heard a
voice saying to it, 'Get up! Devour the flesh of many people!'"
Those who believe this refers to Russia in the last days place
undue emphasis on the modern designation of Russia as the
Bear, which would have been foreign to the original audience. Those who hold this view usually interpret the lion with
wings of an eagle in Daniel 7:4 as a reference to Great Britain
(the lion) and her offspring the United States (the eagle).

However, interpreting ancient prophecies based on modern national symbols is misguided. I, as well as an overwhelming number of Bible commentators, believe the lion in Daniel
7 refers to the ancient Babylonian empire while the bear
refers to the ancient Persian empire. The basis for this interpretation is simple. In Daniel 2, four empires are symbolized
by four metals in a great statue that King Nebuchadnezzar

sees in a dream. The four metals are gold, silver, bronze, and iron. Daniel reveals that the first empire (represented by the head of gold) is Babylon (see Daniel 2:38). Then he says that Babylon will be succeeded by another empire. We know from history that the Medo-Persians followed Babylon, overtaking the city of Babylon in 539 BC. The Persians were followed by Greece and then Rome. Commentators are almost unanimous that the four metals of the statue in Daniel 2 refer to Babylon, Medo-Persia, Greece, and Rome.

The four beasts in Daniel 7:1-7 are parallel to the four metals in Daniel 2, which means the bear in Daniel 7 is not Russia but the ancient Persian empire. We know this because the entire section from Daniel 2–7 is structured as a chiasm, an intentional literary device in which a sequence of ideas is repeated in reverse order, mirroring the original sequence in order to focus attention and highlight the center of the chiasm. Items in a chiasm are parallel, working toward the central point. The chiastic structure reveals that Daniel 2 and 7 cover the same ground, employing different images for the same empires.

CHIASTIC STRUCTURE OF DANIEL 2-7
Daniel 2—World empires symbolized by four metals of a statue
Daniel 3—Three young men delivered from the fiery furnace
Daniel 4—Nebuchadnezzar humbled
Daniel 5—Belshazzar humbled
Daniel 6—Daniel delivered from the lion's den
Daniel 7—World empires symbolized by four wild beasts

Daniel 2 presents the four world empires from man's perspective as a great metallic man, while Daniel 7 views the same empires from God's perspective as wild, ravenous beasts. The bear in Daniel 7:5 is ancient Persia, not Russia.

THE MAGOG CONNECTION

The first place mentioned in Ezekiel 38 is Magog (see Ezekiel 38:2; 39:6).[3] Besides its mention in Ezekiel, the name *Magog* is found in the Bible only in Genesis 10:2 and 1 Chronicles 1:5—where he is listed as a son of Japheth (one of Noah's three sons)—and in Revelation 20:8, a connection we'll examine in chapter 8.[4]

Flavius Josephus, the Jewish historian, says the ancient Scythians inhabited the land of Magog.[5] The Scythians were ruthless northern nomadic tribes who inhabited a large swath of territory encompassing Central Asia and the southern steppes of modern Russia. Magog today includes five former Soviet republics: Kazakhstan, Kyrgyzstan, Uzbekistan, Turkmenistan, and Tajikistan. Afghanistan could also be part of this territory. These nations, with a combined population of more than sixty million, are all Islamic.

Many believe ancient Magog also includes what today is Russia. *The Nelson Study Bible* describes Magog as "usually understood to be in the area near the Black Sea or the Caspian Sea. Magog is one of the sons of Japheth, whose descendants occupied lands from Spain to Asia Minor, the islands of the Mediterranean to southern Russia."[6]

Charles Ryrie says, "*Magog* was identified by Josephus as the land of the Scythians, the region N and NE of the Black Sea and E of the Caspian Sea (now occupied by three members of the Commonwealth of Independent States: Russia, the Ukraine, and Kazakhstan)."[7] Referring to Magog, Rosh, Meshech, and Tubal, Arnold Fruchtenbaum says, "These tribes of the ancient world occupied the areas of modern day Russia."[8] John MacArthur, referring to Ezekiel 38:2, says, "The names of ancient peoples are given who lived in northern Mesopotamia and the Caucasus region of modern Russia."[9]

Ancient Magog included land that today is in Russia.

THE ROSH REFERENCE

After Gog and Magog, the third proper name in Ezekiel 38:2 is Rosh. It's referred to again in Ezekiel 38:3 and 39:1. Because of the obvious similarity of Rosh with Russia, many have equated them. This view was popularized in the note on Ezekiel 38:2 in *The Scofield Reference Bible*: "That the primary reference is to the northern (European) powers, headed up by Russia, all agree. . . . The reference to Meshech and Tubal (Moscow and Tobolsk) is a clear mark of identification."[10]

Scofield seems to base his correlation on the similarity in sound and pronunciation of Rosh, Meshech, and Tubal with Russia, Moscow, and Tobolsk. Linking Rosh in Ezekiel 38:2 and 39:1 with Russia simply because the two words sound similar, however, is not a valid method of interpretation. There is no justification to equate an ancient word with a modern location just because they sound the same. Yet the evidence that Ezekiel was thinking of the land that is now Russia is based on much more than just a similar sound. Three lines of evidence point toward Rosh as Russia.

The Grammar

The language in Ezekiel 38 favors equating Rosh with Russia. The word *rosh* in Hebrew simply means "head, top, summit, or chief." It is a very common word found in all Semitic languages. In the Old Testament alone it appears more than six hundred times. Many English translations of *rosh* render it as the word *chief*, not as the proper name of a geographical location. The King James Version, the Revised Standard Version, the English Standard Version, the New American Bible, and the New International Version all adopt this translation. However, the translation is not unanimous. The Jerusalem Bible, the New English Bible, and the New American Standard Bible all translate *rosh* as a proper name indicating a geographical location.

The preponderance of the evidence supports taking *rosh* as a proper name in Ezekiel chapters 38 and 39. Four main points support this reading. First, the eminent Hebrew scholars C. F. Keil and Wilhelm Gesenius both hold that the superior translation of *rosh* in Ezekiel 38:2-3 and 39:1 is as a proper noun denoting a specific geographical location.[11] Support from these two scholars from the nineteenth century is significant. G. A. Cooke translates Ezekiel 38:2 "the chief of Rosh, Meshech and Tubal." He believes this is "the most natural way of rendering the Hebrew."[12] Nevertheless, many modern translations and commentators translate *rosh* as the adjective "chief," modifying the word "prince." The main reason seems to be that they aren't aware of a place in Ezekiel's day called Rosh. Old Testament scholar John B. Taylor admits that "if place-name Rosh could be vouched for," then Rosh would be the best translation.[13] As we'll discover shortly, a place known as Rosh did exist in Ezekiel's day, thus removing this obstacle to translating *rosh* as a proper name.

Second, in the Septuagint—the Greek translation of the Hebrew Old Testament—*rosh* is translated as the proper name "Ros." While not conclusive, this evidence is weighty in light of the close proximity of the Septuagint to Ezekiel's day. The Septuagint was translated within three centuries of the writing of the book of Ezekiel.[14] The Hebrew Masoretic Text, the basis for most English translations of the Old Testament, also supports taking *rosh* as the name of an ethnic group.[15]

Third, several standard Bible dictionaries and encyclopedias support taking *rosh* as a proper name in Ezekiel 38: *New Bible Dictionary*, *Wycliffe Bible Dictionary*, *Jones' Dictionary of Old Testament Proper Names*, and *Baker Encyclopedia of the Bible*.

Fourth, *rosh* occurs for the first time in Ezekiel 38:2. It appears again in Ezekiel 38:3 and 39:1. C. F. Keil notes that *rosh* must be a proper name since it appears several times because titles are generally abbreviated in Hebrew.[16] If *rosh* were the adjective "chief," it wouldn't reappear two more times.

The biblical evidence strongly supports taking *rosh* as a

proper noun referring to a geographical location. But that's only half of the issue. The next question is—which geographical location? Wilhelm Gesenius, the father of modern Hebrew lexicography, believed Rosh in Ezekiel is a proper name referring to Russia. He wrote in 1846 that Rosh is "undoubtedly the Russians, who are mentioned by the Byzantine writers of the tenth century, under the name Ros, dwelling to the north of Taurus [in Turkey]."[17] Clearly, Gesenius did not base his view on current events or any theological predisposition to favor this view. As author Joel Rosenberg observes,

> What is interesting to me about this assessment is that it was written in 1846, long before the Communist revolution or the subsequent rise of the Soviet Union as a nuclear superpower. In this case, Gesenius was not using a political or economic lens to reach his conclusions. He was using *only* the third lens of Scripture, and the evidence pointed him to Russia more than 160 years ago.[18]

The compelling evidence from biblical scholarship concerning the grammar and language of Ezekiel 38:2 indicates that *rosh* be understood as a proper name, the name of a specific geographic area. Rosh refers to Russia.

The Group of People

One of the arguments against equating Rosh with Russia is that no ancient nation named Rosh existed. However, a growing body of evidence points toward a group of people in the sixth century BC identified as "Rash," "Reshu," or "Ros," who inhabited territory that today is in southern Russia.[19] While the word has a variety of forms and spellings, it is clear that the same people are in view.

Egyptian inscriptions indicate that Rosh existed as early as 2600 BC. A place called Reshu, located north of Egypt, is mentioned in an Egyptian inscription from around 1500 BC.[20] Many other ancient documents mention the place-name *Rosh* in upwards of twenty instances.[21] Rosh was apparently a well-known place in Ezekiel's day. In the sixth century BC, when Ezekiel wrote his prophecy, many of the Rosh people lived in a region north of the Black Sea. After providing extensive evidence of the origin and early history of the Rosh people and then tracing them through the centuries, Clyde Billington concludes,

> As early as 438 A.D., Byzantine Christians placed Gog, Magog, Meshech, Tubal and Ros peoples to the north of Greece in the area that today is Russia. . . . Historical, ethnological, and archaeological evidence all favor the conclusion that the Rosh people of Ezekiel 38–39 were the ancestors of the Rus/Ros people of Europe and Asia. . . . The Rosh people who are mentioned in Ezekiel 38–39 were well-known to ancient and medieval writers by a variety of names which all derived from the names of Tiras and Rosh. . . . Those Rosh people who lived to the

north of the Black Sea in ancient and medieval times were called the Rus/Ros/Rox/Aorsi from very early times. . . . From this mixture with Slavs and with the Varangian Rus in the 9th century, the Rosh people of the area north of the Black Sea formed the people known today as the Russians.[22]

All agree that there is no geographical place today named Rosh. Our task is to identify where the Rosh people lived in Ezekiel's day and then determine what nation occupies that territory today. Arnold Fruchtenbaum writes, "While the names of these geographical areas have changed over the centuries . . . and may change again, the geography itself remains intact. Regardless of what names they may carry at the time of this invasion, it is these very geographical areas that are involved. Although the leading nation may have once been called the Soviet Union, and more recently the Commonwealth of Independent States, and traditionally Russia, it is this territory—by whatever name it may be called at that time—that will lead this invasion."[23]

The Geography

The third main line of evidence for identifying Rosh as Russia is based on location. Ezekiel chapters 38 and 39 emphasize repeatedly that at least part of this last-days' invading force will come "from the distant north" (38:6, 15; 39:2). Biblical directions are usually given in reference to Israel, which on God's compass is the "center" (or "navel") of the earth (see

Ezekiel 38:12, NASB). This valuable textual clue points to Russia. If you draw a line directly north from Israel on a map, only five nations are in line: Lebanon, Syria, Turkey, Ukraine, and Russia. But the one farthest north is Russia.[24] John Walvoord says, "One cannot escape Russia if he goes north of the Holy Land. On the basis of geography alone, it seems quite clear that the only nation which could possibly be referred to as coming from the far north would be the nation Russia."[25]

Paul Enns notes, "These enemies come from the 'remote parts of the north' (vv. 6, 15), modern Turkey and southern Russia—the nations surrounding the Black and Caspian Seas."[26]

Walter Kaiser is unsure if Rosh in Ezekiel 38 is Russia, but he sees the geographical reference to the far north as unmistakable. "They are depicted by Ezekiel as 'coming from [their] place in the far north' (15). The allusion to the 'far north' also points to a Russian-led confederation, for Moscow is almost directly north of Jerusalem on a modern map."[27]

Based on geography, Scripture indicates Russia will be the leader of the northern coalition of the end times.

THE BEAR NECESSITY

To further support the presence of Russia in Ezekiel 38, I thought it would be helpful to briefly quote a few other reliable sources who have studied this issue extensively. Charles Dyer and Mark Tobey say, "Most Bible students with even cursory understanding of biblical prophecy suspect that Russia will play some strategic role in end-time events."[28] Charles Dyer, in his commentary on Ezekiel, is even more specific: "Some of the countries named by Ezekiel were located in what is now Russia."[29] Speaking of Ezekiel 38, Lamar Cooper says, "The geographical area would today include . . . southern provinces of Russia."[30] Theologian Charles Ryrie says, "The land of Russia looms large and menacing in Ezekiel's prophetic picture."[31] Dr. David Jeremiah writes, "Approximately twenty-five hundred years ago, Ezekiel predicted Russia's return to power in the latter days."[32]

Popular Bible teacher J. Vernon McGee describes how he came to his view:

> When I first entered the ministry, I took the position that these two chapters of Ezekiel could not possibly speak of the modern nation of Russia under any circumstances. Even when I began seminary work on my Th.M. and Th.D., I did not accept that interpretation. I began to study on my own and attempt to arrive at a decision—whether or not this could possibly be Russia. Now I am convinced beyond a shadow of a doubt that chapters 38 and 39 refer to Russia.[33]

J. Dwight Pentecost, a preeminent prophecy scholar, authored his classic work *Things to Come* in 1958 and noted, "The identification of Rosh as modern Russia would seem to be well authenticated and generally accepted."[34] Joel Rosenberg concludes,

> The words *Russia, Moscow, Soviet Union,* and *czar* never appear in these passages [Ezekiel 38–39]. Nor do they appear anywhere in the book of Ezekiel. Nor are they ever mentioned anywhere in the Bible. But there is no doubt that the ancient prophet was referring to the nation we now know as Russia. . . . Based on the textual, linguistic, and historical evidence, we can . . . conclude with a high degree of confidence that Ezekiel is speaking of Russia and the former Soviet Union in chapters 38 and 39.[35]

These authors and scholars are far from alone in their assessment. Many, many more well-respected scholars, pastors, commentators, and popular Bible teachers could be cited who believe Ezekiel 38 refers to Russia and its allies. Of course, their support for this view doesn't prove it's correct, but it should demonstrate that this is not a fringe, fanatical view.

HISTORY, NOT HEADLINES

Contemporary writers aren't the only ones who believe Ezekiel chapters 38 and 39 refer to Russia. This view has a long line of support. I make this point because one repeated objection to identifying Magog or Rosh with Russia is that this is nothing more than "sensationalistic end-time specula-tion" based on the current headlines.[36] While there is cer-tainly unwarranted speculation and newspaper exegesis by some prophecy teachers, contemporary scholars are not alone in their appraisal that Rosh and Magog in Ezekiel 38 refer to Russia.

Here's a brief list of scholars from previous generations who identified Rosh or Magog with Russia:

- Matthew Henry, in his famous commentary written in the early 1700s, was aware of some who identified Russia with Ezekiel 38. He says, "Some think they find them afar off, in Scythia, Tartary, and Russia."[37] Henry doesn't say he agrees with the view, but his awareness of it demonstrates that it at least was not uncommon.
- Patrick Fairbairn, a Scottish Presbyterian preacher, in his 1842 commentary on Ezekiel, notes that Rosh is a reference to Russia.[38]
- Jamieson, Fausset, and Brown, commenting on Rosh in Ezekiel 38 in 1871, says, "The Scythian Tauri in the Crimea were so called. The Araxes also was called 'Rhos.' The modern Russians may have hence *assumed* their name" (emphasis added).[39]
- William Kelly, a Plymouth Brethren scholar, writing in 1876, identifies Gog (the leader of the invasion in Ezekiel 38) by noting, "He is autocrat of all the Russias, prince of Rosh, Meshech, and Tubal."[40] He

writes, "Next follow two chapters which contain a prediction of God's judgment to fall in the last days, when Israel is restored, on a great north-eastern chief with his vast array of satellites and allies on the mountains of the Holy Land. . . . Who can deny that the rapid and immense development of the Russian empire bears its unmistakable witness to the judgment that is coming, as here declared so long before?"[41]

- Arno Gaebelein, writing in the early twentieth century, says, "The leader is the prince of Rosh. . . . And here we call attention to the prince, this northern leader, or king, who is the head of all these nations. He is the prince of Rosh. Careful research has established the fact that the progenitor of Rosh was Tiraz [Genesis 10:2], and that Rosh is Russia. All students of prophecy are agreed that this is the correct meaning of Rosh. The prince of Rosh, means, therefore, the prince or king of the Russian empire."[42]

Studying the Word of God, not current events or headlines, formed the views of these scholars. We seek to follow their example. God's Word must be our guide. The fact that current events are aligning with what Scripture says does not render this view sensationalism. Rather, it demonstrates the truth of Scripture and points toward the coming of Christ.

CONCLUSION

Ezekiel 38 reveals that Russia will rise in the last days as a formidable global power. Whether or not one sees Rosh or Magog as Russia, the far northern geographical notation is clear. The rise of Russia today is no coincidence; it's divine providence. Events happening in Russia today strikingly foreshadow Ezekiel's ancient prophecy. Russian tentacles reach around the world. The buildup toward a Middle East war is accelerating. The Bear is rising to take its place among the cast of characters in the final drama of the ages. But Russia will not rise alone. Ezekiel lists a group of allies who will conspire with Russia's leader for a final push into the Middle East—into the land of Israel. These nations dominate today's headlines and are presently forming alliances with Russia.

Who are these allies?

The *Who's Who* of Middle Eastern bad actors.

CHAPTER 4

EZEKIEL'S PROPHETIC INTELLIGENCE BRIEFING

YOU WILL COME FROM YOUR HOMELAND IN THE DISTANT NORTH WITH YOUR VAST CAVALRY AND YOUR MIGHTY ARMY.

EZEKIEL 38:15

As we saw in the last chapter, when we carefully examine the text of Ezekiel 38, we can see that in the end times a Russian leader will spearhead an attack on Israel. But Ezekiel 38 also reveals that Russia will not mount this attack alone. Who will join them? Ezekiel "provides us extraordinarily precise intelligence," Joel Rosenberg writes. "Though he wrote more than 2,500 years ago, the Hebrew prophet was able to tell us what to watch for."[1] Incredibly, all the way back in 586 BC, Ezekiel peered into the future and gave us an intelligence briefing for who will join Russia in their anti-Israel assault.

The first thing Ezekiel does is give a detailed list of the participants in the Russian-led coalition:

1. Gog
2. Magog
3. Rosh
4. Meshech
5. Tubal
6. Persia
7. Ethiopia (Cush)
8. Libya (Put)
9. Gomer
10. Beth-togarmah

Pause for a moment and read these verses to get the context in view:

> This is another message that came to me from the LORD: "Son of man, turn and face Gog of the land of Magog, the prince who rules over* the nations of Meshech and Tubal, and prophesy against him. Give him this message from the Sovereign LORD: Gog, I am your enemy! I will turn you around and put hooks in your jaws to lead you out with your whole army—your horses and charioteers in full armor and a great horde armed with shields and swords. Persia,

---

* The New Living Translation translates the Hebrew *rosh* as "who rules over." See the discussion in the last chapter, where I make the case that the better translation is "Rosh," a proper noun/nation (as in NASB).

Ethiopia, and Libya will join you, too, with all their weapons. Gomer and all its armies will also join you, along with the armies of Beth-togarmah from the distant north, and many others.

"Get ready; be prepared! Keep all the armies around you mobilized, and take command of them."

EZEKIEL 38:1-7

Before we examine the location names listed in Ezekiel 38:1-6, I want to briefly comment on the principle of interpretation we'll employ. More and more scholars and commentators today opt for a general or even spiritualizing approach to the prophecy of Ezekiel 38 and many other prophetic Scriptures.[2] Interestingly, those who adopt this approach usually take the geographical references in Ezekiel 1–32 to refer to literal places and people, yet when they come to the final chapters of Ezekiel, they shift to a spiritualizing approach, claiming that these chapters are "apocalyptic" and justify a shift in interpretive method. Much could be said about this practice, but at the very least it's inconsistent. Nothing in Ezekiel chapters 38 and 39 signals these chapters are to be understood in any way other than literal. The method of interpretation is the same for the whole book of Ezekiel. Charles Feinberg spotlights an important interpretive guideline:

> Some suggest a "generally literal" interpretation where the details are not necessarily so. The writer cannot

allow himself such liberties in interpreting the plain statements of the prophetic Scriptures. It is either the grammatical, literal, historical interpretation or we are adrift on an uncharted sea with every man the norm for himself. There is not a syllable at the beginning of this chapter to alert us to explain the passage in any other than the literal method.[3]

The best approach, in my opinion, is to understand these chapters as referring to actual places and people that will appear on the world scene in the last days, just as the text says.

Ezekiel 38 describes a coalition of nations, listing each of the nations by its ancient place-name in Ezekiel's day. But before he unveils the nations that will join Russia in this military offensive, Ezekiel identifies the commander of this horde.

THE COMMANDER

The leader of the first great war of the end times is called "Gog of the land of Magog, the prince of Rosh, Meshech and Tubal" (Ezekiel 38:2, NASB). The name *Gog*, which occurs ten times in the New Living Translation of Ezekiel 38–39, is the name or title of the leader of the invasion. We know this because he is directly addressed by God (see 38:14; 39:1), called a prince (see 38:2; 39:1), and repeatedly referred to by the use of personal pronouns. Also, he is "of the land of Magog," indicating he is an individual. The word *Gog* is likely not the leader's name but serves as a title like "pharaoh," "president," or "czar."

In the Old Testament, the word *Gog* appears only one time outside Ezekiel 38–39—in 1 Chronicles 5:4—but clearly in reference to a different person. *Gog* may mean "high" or "supreme," or it may represent a height, possibly emphasizing this leader's elevated position and pride. The word *Gog* may come from the Sumerian word *gug*, meaning "darkness."

The name *Gog* has been identified with many personages both ancient and modern. Here are some of the more common views:

- Gog is Gugu or Gyges, a Lydian king in the seventh century BC. (Lydia is part of the modern nation of Turkey.)
- Gog is a cryptogram or code name for Babylon.
- Gog is another name for the end-times Antichrist.
- Gog is a symbolic term for any enemy of God.

I don't believe Gog and the Antichrist should be equated. According to Daniel 7 and Revelation 13, the final Antichrist will lead the Western confederacy of nations, reunited out of the old Roman empire, while Gog is from Russia and leads a primarily northern force. Daniel 11:40 calls the Russian leader "the king of the north." Gog and the Antichrist are two different leaders who are in opposition to each other.

The best view seems to be that Gog is a title for the ruler of Russia derived from a recent ruler in Ezekiel's day (Gyges or Gugu) that Ezekiel employs to describe the character of the final Russian ruler. Charles Dyer and Mark Tobey hold this view. They believe Gog is "most likely an allusion to an ancient king named Gyges who died about seventy years before Ezekiel delivered his prophecy. By identifying this still-future ruler as 'Gog,' Ezekiel was using someone from his recent past to paint a one-word portrait of this future ruler. It is similar to someone today identifying the future Antichrist as the next 'Hitler' or 'Stalin'—men who also died several decades ago but whose evil legacy is still fresh on people's minds."[4] Whatever specific view one takes of the meaning of Gog, Ezekiel is clear that he will be the northern commander of this last-days coalition.

THE COALITION

The name *Gog* is followed by nine ancient place-names. Our task is to decode these ancient locations and identify their modern counterparts.

The Table of Nations in Genesis 10 helps us with this task because all the names in Ezekiel 38 (save Rosh) are listed there as the descendants of Noah's sons Shem, Ham, and especially Japheth. In locating these places today, we need to remember that Ezekiel used the names for these places that were familiar in his day (ca. 593–570 BC). The names of these places have changed many times over the millennia and may change again before this prophecy is fulfilled. Nevertheless, these are the geographical locations, whatever their names may be, that will be part of this massive Russian-led incursion into Israel in the last days. Paul Enns observes, "The names *Gog*, *Rosh*, *Meshech*, and *Tubal* were historic names that should be understood *representatively* or *eschatologically*. Ezekiel prophesied concerning a future invasion against Israel, but used names of nations during his day because the future invaders would be from the same geographical places."[5]

In the last chapter we looked at the evidence that identifies Rosh as Russia, so we won't go over that same ground again, but we'll identify the other eight places Ezekiel pinpoints.

Magog

Magog was the second son of Japheth and the grandson of Noah. The name *Magog* is found elsewhere in Scripture in Genesis 10:2, 1 Chronicles 1:5, Ezekiel 39:6, and Revelation 20:8. We discussed Magog in the last chapter in some detail and discovered that many identify Magog as Russia and/ or the Islamic nations of Central Asia, possibly including Afghanistan. Again, Charles Ryrie notes that Magog "was identified . . . as the land of the Scythians . . . now occupied by . . . Russia, the Ukraine, and Kazakhstan."[6] Magog is the land of the ancient Scythians and encompasses the Central Asian nations that formed the underbelly of the Soviet Union. These predominantly Muslim nations have a combined population of more than sixty million. Robbed of these nations and longing for a return to the Soviet empire, Russia is working to woo them back under its umbrella. The

Eurasian Economic Union is strongly supported by Russia to extend its influence in Central Asia.

Meshech and Tubal

Meshech and Tubal are normally mentioned together in Scripture (see Ezekiel 27:13; 32:26). C. I. Scofield identifies Meshech and Tubal as the Russian cities of Moscow and Tobolsk.[7]

Over the years many others have followed Scofield's identification. The names of these places do sound alike, but as I mentioned in the last chapter, this by itself is not a proper method of identifying the current locations of these ancient places. The context of the book of Ezekiel rules out any association of these places with Moscow or Tobolsk. Meshech and Tubal are mentioned as trading partners with ancient Tyre, which is modern Lebanon (see Ezekiel 27:13). Ezekiel 32:26 records their recent defeat by their enemies. Ancient records provide no credible evidence that Tyre was trading with places as remote as Moscow and the Siberian city of Tobolsk. Also, Ezekiel would certainly not have been aware of any defeat of armies that distant from Israel.

The more reliable identification is that Meshech is the ancient *Moschoi* in Greek writing and *Musku* in Assyrian inscriptions, while Tubal is *Tibarenoi* and *Tabal*. Both of these locations are in present-day Turkey, a nation that is strengthening ties with Russia and Iran.

Gomer

Like Magog, Meshech, and Tubal, Gomer was a son of Japheth. He was the first son of Japheth and the grandson of Noah (see Genesis 10:2-3). Many have identified Gomer as Germany. Arnold Fruchtenbaum says, "Gomer . . . [is] located in present-day Germany. This too was the rabbinic view. The *Midrash* calls Gomer *Germania* and that is also the way the *Talmud* refers to Gomer."[8] In the days of the Cold War and the Iron Curtain, when Eastern Europe was under Soviet control, Gomer was often identified with East Germany. John Phillips believes Gomer refers to Germany and speculates, "What if a united and anti-Semitic Germany were to seek its future fortunes while allied to an anti-Semitic Russia?"[9] If true, that would be a formidable partnership.

While Gomer could refer to modern Germany, since the ancient Gomerites migrated from their original home in the area of modern Turkey to other locations, the more likely connection is with Turkey. That's where the Gomerites resided in Ezekiel's day.

Ancient Gomer was referred to by the Assyrians as the *Gimirrai* and by the Greeks as the *Cimmerians*. They emerged in the eighth century BC in the area of Asia Minor, or modern Turkey. Later, in the first century AD, the Jewish historian Josephus connected the Gomerites with the Galatians, who inhabited what today is central Turkey.[10]

Turkey is an Islamic nation, and under the influence of President Erdoğan it is throwing off its secular leanings and embracing its Islamic roots from the days of the Ottoman empire. With growing ties to Russia and Iran, Turkey exerts a growing political and military influence on events in the Middle East.

Persia

After the mention of the northern threat from Russia and Turkey, the next future member of the Russian coalition in the War of Gog and Magog is Persia. The words *Persia*, *Persian*, or *Persians* are found more than thirty times in the Old Testament. In Ezekiel 38:5, Persia is best understood as modern-day Iran. The ancient land of Persia became the modern nation of Iran in March 1935, and then the name was changed to the Islamic Republic of Iran in 1979. Walter Kaiser states, "It is interesting to note that the nation of Iran (which includes present-day Pakistan and Afghanistan as well) gets first mention and that most of Gog's allies are countries that are today predominantly Islamic."[11]

Iran's present population is almost eighty million. Iran's mullah regime is the world's number-one sponsor of terror and is making its bid for regional supremacy at the same time it is pursuing nuclear weapons. Iran's venomous hatred of Israel is no secret.

The agreement with Iran brokered by the United States appears to be a bad deal. The deal does delay Iran getting its hands on nukes, but only for ten years. After ten years, all bets are off, and Iran will be free to cross the nuclear finish line. Time will tell whether the Iran deal was successful. But we do know that Iran is now out from under crippling sanctions and had more than $100 billion returned to its coffers to further fund its terrorist proxies.

Iran is a nuclear-threshold state with a breakout capacity of less than one year. Iran's compliance with the US agreement is not always easy to verify, so the likelihood of cheating is ever present. All the while, Iran is conducting ballistic missile tests and has three underground ballistic missile factories. Nuclear capability in Iran combined with ballistic missiles raises a sum-of-all-fears scenario. Clearly, modern Iran is a country hostile to Israel and the West. We'll deal more in depth with Iran in the next chapter.

Ethiopia (Cush)

Two North African nations are listed in Ezekiel 38. The first is Ethiopia, which translates the Hebrew word *Cush*. Ancient Cush was called *Kusu* by the Assyrians and Babylonians, *Kos* or *Kas* by the Egyptians, and *Nubia* by the Greeks. Secular history locates Cush directly south of ancient Egypt, extending down past the modern city of Khartoum, which is the capital of modern Sudan. Modern Sudan inhabits the ancient land of Cush.

Sudan was locked in a deadly struggle between the Islamic north and Christian south for decades, culminating with South Sudan announcing its independence in July 2011. Since then, Sudan has been split into two sovereign nations. Northern Sudan, known simply as "Sudan" or officially as "the Republic of the Sudan," is a militant, radical Islamic nation that supported Iraq and its leader Saddam Hussein in the Gulf War. The Sudanese government invited Osama bin Laden and his deputy Ayman al-Zawahiri to Sudan and became a safe haven for jihadists. Osama bin Laden was sheltered there from 1991 to 1996. It should be no surprise that Sudan appears in this list of Russian allies against Israel and the West in the end times. Sudan would jump at the opportunity to take its place with Russia in the coming Gog alliance, just as Ezekiel predicted.

Libya (Put)

Put was a son of Ham (see Genesis 10:6). Josephus identified Put as Libya. The ancient *Babylonian Chronicles* reveal that *Putu* was the distant land to the west of Egypt, which we know as Libya and could possibly include nations farther west, such as modern Algeria and Tunisia. The Greek translation of the Old Testament renders the word *Put* as *Libues*.

Modern Libya remains a hardened Islamic state that hates Israel and despises the West. Strongman Muammar al-Qaddafi exercised a reign of terror over Libya from 1969 until he was killed in 2011 in an Arab Spring eruption that spread to Libya. After the collapse of his government and his death, Libya fragmented and quickly fell into disarray, with various fighting factions vying for power. ISIS seized the opportunity and moved in to fill some of the vacuum. Many fear Libya may end up in a morass like Somalia, which is a dangerous, chaotic land of pirates and warlords. A steady stream of desperate refugees is fleeing the chaos.

In recent days, Russia has begun to exert greater influence in Libya. Russia has deployed troops near the Libyan border. Recent headlines unveil the strengthening ties between Russia and Libya:

"Global Insights: Russia's Libya Strategy"

WORLD POLITICS REVIEW, APRIL 12, 2011

"Russia Enlarges Military Footprint in Libya"

UPI.COM, MARCH 20, 2017

"Russia Makes Play for Libya"

LIBERTY UNYIELDING, MARCH 18, 2017

"Has Moscow Found Its New Gadhafi in Libya?"

REAL CLEAR WORLD, MARCH 24, 2017

"Russian Warship Hosts Libya's Haftar as Putin Courts New Ally"

BLOOMBERG, JANUARY 11, 2017

A crucial result of the Syrian war is that Russia is now emboldened. Russia has an increasing military presence in Libya, supporting Libyan Field Marshal Khalifa Haftar in the ongoing civil conflict that has engulfed that nation.[12] Haftar is a former colonel in the army of Libyan leader Muammar al-Qaddafi. "While testifying to the Senate's foreign relations committee, the chief of the Pentagon's Africa command, General Thomas D. Waldhauser, said, 'Russia is trying to exert influence on the ultimate decision of who and what entity becomes in charge of the government inside Libya.'"[13]

Libya is in place for the coming Middle East war led by Russia.

Beth-togarmah

Togarmah was the third son of Gomer, who was a son of Japheth (see Genesis 10:3). Ezekiel 38:6 states that the armies of Beth-togarmah, from the distant north, will join the Russian alliance.

Beth-togarmah is referenced in Ezekiel 27:14 as a trading partner of Tyre (modern Lebanon). Ancient Beth-togarmah was called *Til-garamu* by the Assyrians and *Tegarma* by the Hittites. Both the Assyrians and Hittites located Beth-togarmah in what is modern-day Turkey, along with Meshech, Tubal, and Gomer.

THE COMING COALITION

Thomas Constable puts the pieces of this coalition together, showing how the players come from every direction:

Persia lay to Israel's northeast, Ethiopia to her
southwest, Put to her southeast (on the African coast

of the southern Red Sea), Gomer to her northwest (in the Taurus mountains of Anatolia and possibly farther northwest in modern western Europe), and Beth-togarmah to her northwest (southeast of the Black Sea). Thus peoples all around Israel would unite against her under Gog's leadership. As Babylonia sought to destroy Israel in the past, so this latter-day Babylon will seek to destroy her in the future.[14]

THE GOG COALITION	
Ancient Name	**Modern Location**
Rosh	Russia
Magog (Scythians)	Central Asia and possibly Afghanistan
Meshech	Turkey
Tubal	Turkey
Persia	Iran
Ethiopia (Cush)	Sudan
Libya (Put)	Libya
Gomer	Turkey
Beth-togarmah	Turkey

Ezekiel 38–39 predicts a Russian-led invasion of the land of Israel in the last days by an alliance of nations collapsing on Israel from every direction. Russia will be joined by five main allies: Turkey, Iran, Libya, Sudan, and the Islamic nations

of the former Soviet Union. Increasingly, these nations are hotbeds of radical Islam and are either forming or consolidating their bonds with Russia and each other. This list of nations could be taken from the headlines of any newspaper or Internet news source. Envisioning these nations coming together under Russian leadership to attack Israel and trigger a Middle East war is not far-fetched.

Seven times throughout Ezekiel 38–39 the words "thus says the Lord God" appear.[15] Ezekiel's prophecy claims to be the very word of God himself. The detail of this ancient prophecy is also an ironclad proof that this claim is true. Think about it. More than 2,500 years ago, the prophet Ezekiel named each of these specific nations that we read about in the news every day. This degree of detail and specificity validates the uniqueness of the Bible as the Word of the living God.

Ezekiel 37 predicts the regathering and restoration of the Jewish people to their ancient homeland, which began in 1948 with the rebirth of the modern state of Israel. This astounding prophecy is being fulfilled before our eyes. God's Word is coming to pass. Immediately after Ezekiel 37, the prophet predicts the rise of the Gog coalition. The consolidation of these nations will be literally fulfilled, just like Ezekiel 37, and we're already seeing its foreshadowing. The convergence of these events is no happenstance. No one but an all-knowing, all-powerful God could make predictions like this.

MISSING IN ACTION

As we've made our way through this list of nations, you might be asking, "What about the other Middle East nations not included here—nations like Egypt, Syria, Jordan, Lebanon, Saudi Arabia, and Iraq? Do we know anything about their future? Could they play some role in the events of Ezekiel 38?"

Ezekiel's list focuses on Israel's remote enemies, the outer ring of nations from every direction—Russia, Central Asia, Iran, Turkey, Sudan, and Libya. The near enemies or inner ring of nations that encircle Israel are conspicuously absent from the litany of nations for the War of Gog and Magog. Two plausible answers for this omission have been suggested.

First, these near nations may not be mentioned because they have suffered defeat at some earlier point and been neutralized. That's the thesis of prophecy teachers who posit a "Psalm 83 war" that they believe precedes the War of Gog and Magog. Psalm 83 describes the nations surrounding Israel "sign[ing] a treaty as allies against [God]" (verse 5), with the psalmist asking God to intervene, to "utterly disgrace them until they submit to your name, O LORD" (verse 16). During this war, these prophecy teachers contend that Israel will defeat its near enemies and emerge from the war with renewed military prowess and peace, setting the stage for Ezekiel 38–39.

While this view is certainly a possible explanation, the main drawback for a Psalm 83 war is that the Jewish prophets are silent about it. A Psalm 83 war would be a momentous event on God's prophetic calendar, and it seems strange to me that any mention of it would be missing from the prophets. Moreover, Psalm 83 is a lament psalm, lacking any chronological specifics concerning when it will be fulfilled. Any suggestion for when it will be fulfilled is based on speculation, not the psalm itself. In contrast, the War of Gog and Magog contains several chronological indicators.[16] For these reasons, I reject the idea of a separate Psalm 83 war.

The second possibility, and in my view a better explanation, is that the inner ring of nations around Israel could be part of the invasion but not specifically mentioned. At the very end of Ezekiel 38:6, after listing the specific allies in this assault force, Ezekiel adds, "and many others." I believe this general statement refers to the closer nations surrounding Israel that are not specifically mentioned by Ezekiel. The nations mentioned in Ezekiel 38:1-6 are distant, remote enemies of Israel from every direction. Ezekiel's addition of the words "and many others" at the end of his list includes the near enemies of Israel that live within the outer circle of far enemies. Walter Kaiser supports this view: "There seems also to be many other nations not mentioned, but who are fully allied with Gog."[17]

The mountains of Israel are mentioned three times (see Ezekiel 38:8; 39:2, 4). While forming a spine down its middle, Israel's mountains are mainly found in the north, near Israel's border with Syria and Lebanon. This area is known as the Golan Heights. The Russian-led invasion will come primarily from the north and seems to be focused on the mountains of Israel, so it's not hard to imagine that Syria and Lebanon could participate in this invasion.[18]

Egypt, the end-times king of the south, will probably be a part of this invasion as well. Egypt's inclusion is derived from Daniel 11:40, which predicts a coalition between the king of the north (Russia and the northern allies) and the king of the south, which points to an end-times leader of Egypt joined by the other North African nations in Ezekiel 38. The reason Ezekiel 38 omits Egypt from its list is probably because Ezekiel 38 focuses on the far enemies. The parallel passage in Daniel 11:40 fills in the total picture.[19]

Egypt has enjoyed peaceful relations with Israel since 1978, when Menachem Begin and Anwar Sadat signed the Camp David Accords. But Egypt must turn against Israel for Daniel 11:40 to be fulfilled. Years ago Henry Kissinger said that no war in the Middle East is possible without Egypt.[20] While Kissinger's statement may not always hold true, Egypt will lead the North African contingent in the end times.

As you can see, Russia will pull together a colossal coalition in the end of days.

THE DISSENTERS

All signs in our world today point toward the fulfillment of Ezekiel 38–39. Russia and its allies seem to be far down the road that eventually leads to Israel. But not every nation in the end times will support this invasion. Ezekiel highlights a group of nations that will lodge a protest, albeit a lame one, to this military offensive. The opposition is described in Ezekiel 38:13: "Sheba and Dedan and the merchants of Tarshish will ask, 'Do you really think the armies you have gathered can rob them of silver and gold? Do you think you can drive away their livestock and seize their goods and carry off plunder?'"

Notice that these nations don't *do* anything; they just question what's happening. Their mild protest doesn't change anything. They question the motivation and purpose of the invasion. This looks frighteningly similar to the passive reaction we often see from the United Nations and nations in the West to international aggression.

Three specific places are listed as the source of the opposition—Sheba, Dedan, and Tarshish. Sheba and Dedan are easy to identify. They refer to nations on the Arabian Peninsula and along the Persian Gulf. Walter Kaiser notes that Sheba and Dedan are usually identified with people "living in the Arabian peninsula, including Saudi Arabia, Yemen, Oman, Kuwait, and the United Arab Emirates."[21] Most of these nations are under moderate Sunni Arab regimes who oppose the more militant strains of Islam.[22]

Tarshish is more difficult to identify with precision. The identification is complicated by the mention of "all its villages" (NASB) or "all the young lions" (KJV). Arnold Fruchtenbaum notes, "This phrase is a Hebrew idiom meaning nations that have come out of Tarshish."[23] But the real issue is the location of Tarshish itself. Two places in the ancient world are identified as Tarshish—Spain and England. If Tarshish is Spain, the nations that came from it include "Central and South America, except for Brazil."[24] If the location is England, it would include the United States, Canada, Australia, and New Zealand.

The name *Tarshish* was used in ancient times to denote the farthest lands to the west, so it's probably best to identify Tarshish as the western nations of Europe and possibly even the United States, although the US connection is more tenuous.

The lack of any mention of international support for Israel, other than this weak protest, means that by the time of the Russian invasion, the United States will be either unwilling or unable to do anything to help. There are many plausible scenarios that could explain US absence in Bible prophecy, but clearly the Rapture—the instantaneous vanishing of all believers as they are taken up to heaven (recorded in 1 Thessalonians 4:15-17)—would leave the United States severely weakened and possibly a second-rate world power.

Regardless of the exact location of Tarshish or of what role, if any, the United States will play, these nations in Ezekiel 38:13 will resist Russia and its allies but only with words. Israel's only help will come from God.

THE CLOCK IS TICKING

The pieces of Ezekiel's prophecy seem to be moving into place. Russia and the allies outlined in Ezekiel 38 are identifiable nations with the intent and incentive to join together and attack Israel. Even the nations that will object to this foray are viable nations with competing interests against Russia and its radical partners.

The rise of Russia under Vladimir Putin and the formation of new alliances is another sign indicating the Lord's coming may be very soon. As Joel Rosenberg says,

> Whether he realizes the prophetic implications of his actions or not, Putin has clearly embarked upon an aggressive and systematic effort to build new alliances with countries specifically cited in Ezekiel 38–39, as well as with those countries that could be involved in the War of Gog and Magog but are not clearly defined in the text. And the clock is ticking.
>
> So watch closely, for such efforts will only intensify as the time of Ezekiel's vision comes to fulfillment.[25]

I like the story about a bunch of sailors who were returning from a long voyage away from home. As the boat approached shore, the men were all looking eagerly for their wives and girlfriends on the dock. As the men scanned the crowd of women lining the railing, the air of excitement and expectancy grew. One man, however, was all alone as he watched all the other men find their wives and girlfriends, and they all embraced. But his wife was nowhere to be found. Worried, he hurried home and found a light on in his house. As he entered he was relieved to see his wife. She quickly turned and said, "Honey, I've been waiting for you." His response displayed his deep disappointment. "The other men's wives and girlfriends were *watching* for them!"

Are we just *waiting* for Jesus, or are we *watching* for him? Are we watching closely?

The clock is ticking.

Live looking!

CHAPTER 5

TRIPLE THREAT: RUSSIA, IRAN, AND TURKEY

A TECTONIC SHIFT HAS OCCURRED IN THE BALANCE OF POWER IN THE MIDDLE EAST. . . . TURKEY AND IRAN ARE SIMULTANEOUSLY MOVING TOWARD RUSSIA, WHILE RUSSIA IS EXPANDING ITS GLOBAL MILITARY AND STRATEGIC REACH. . . . THIS WILL HAVE A MAJOR IMPACT ACROSS THE REGION, POTENTIALLY LEAVING U.S. ALLY ISRAEL ISOLATED TO FACE A MASSIVE HOSTILE ALLIANCE ARMED WITH NUCLEAR WEAPONS.

KENNETH R. TIMMERMAN

As we saw in the last chapter, Ezekiel 38:1-6 lists ten proper names, identifying the leader and the nations that will launch an offensive against Israel in the latter years. At least seven, and possibly eight, of the ten names refer to the leader of Russia and the modern nations of Russia, Turkey, and Iran. These three nations form the central core of the northern coalition led by the king of the north.

All three of these nations are emerging at the same time and forging stronger ties to one another. Any news watcher, no matter how casual, knows that these three countries find themselves in the headlines almost every day.

In the case of Russia, the Kremlin has accused Americans of having an "emotional obsession" with Russia in light of US allegations of election hacking and meddling and collusion.[1]

Iran's open pursuit of nuclear weapons, numerous ballistic missile tests, and the Obama administration's controversial Iran nuclear deal keep it front and center.

Turkey's controversial referendum vote in April 2017, which gives President Erdoğan almost unilateral control over his country, has perplexed and worried the world.

The horrible Syrian conflict and the rise of ISIS have put the Russia-Iran-Turkey axis in the daily news.

The rise of a Russian-Iranian-Turkish triumvirate is a hugely significant development both historically and prophetically. Historically, these nations share a fascinating, common feature: "All three were empires long before they became nation-states."[2] Each had its turn dominating the region and basking in glory, but each has lost much of the territory it previously controlled:

- Persian empire (550–331 BC)
- Ottoman empire (AD 1299–1923)
- Russian empire created by Peter the Great (1721–1917)
- Soviet empire (1917–1991)

In its own way, each of these nations seems to be driven to recover its former glory. To one degree or another, each also feels snubbed by Western powers and holds a smoldering resentment against them. Their shared historical experience, while not the sole explanation for their ties, may play some role in their sharing headlines.

Russia and Iran are already in Syria, right on Israel's northern border. Turkey is in the mix in the Syrian civil war and the war on ISIS. World news takes notice of the growing alignment of these three allies, especially in relation to the war in Syria.

"An Inevitable Triumvirate: Syria, Russia, and Iran"

FOREIGN POLICY IN FOCUS, OCTOBER 15, 2015

"Why Russia, Turkey and Iran Are Natural Allies"

THE CONVERSATION, JANUARY 5, 2017

"Syria and the Complex Geostrategic Game of Russia-Turkey-Iran"

MIDDLE EAST BRIEFING, JANUARY 12, 2017

"Russia, Iran, Turkey to Enforce Cease-Fire in Syria"

UPI, JANUARY 24, 2017

"Syrian Safe Zones Plan Goes into Effect after Deal by Russia, Turkey, Iran"

CHICAGO TRIBUNE, MAY 5, 2017

"Russia, Iran and Turkey Meet for Syria Talks, Excluding U.S."

NEW YORK TIMES, DECEMBER 20, 2016

Russia, Iran, and Turkey inhabit the same neighborhood and share many common interests, yet the Syrian conflict that began in 2011 has pulled them closer than ever. At the same time that Turkey is becoming more distanced from the West and Iran's alienation has pushed them further into the Russian orbit, the Syrian civil war is a driving force in uniting these nations. Russia and Iran both support the brutal regime of Syrian president Bashar al-Assad against the US-supported rebels.

Russia, Iran, and Turkey are getting closer to one another in Syria and very close to Israel's northern border. The framework for ending the Syrian conflict, known as "the Moscow Declaration," was accepted by Russia, Iran, and Turkey. Christian Caryl of the *Washington Post* writes, "While Moscow, Ankara and Tehran plot their own 'peace process' for the Syrian civil war, the United States is conspicuous in its absence."[3] Washington's reticence has created a vacuum, and these powers are all too willing to fill it.

RUSSIAN RESURGENCE

We've discussed current events in Russia and Russia's future quite a bit already, so let's just touch on a couple of ways Russia is allying itself with Iran and Turkey.

In spite of past differences and disagreements, Russia and Turkey are finding an alliance to be in their mutual interest. The growing ties between Turkey and Russia are to the point that Turkey may be buying advanced defense systems from Russia.

Concerning Iran, "Russia launched a fleet of bombers bound for Syria . . . from an Iranian air base, becoming the first foreign military to operate from Iran's soil since at least World War II."[4] Putin has praised Iran's leader as a "reliable and stable partner."[5]

Putin announced that trade between Russia and Iran rose 70 percent from 2016 to 2017. Russia and Iran "signed more than a dozen agreements on economics, tourism, diplomacy and other issues" in March 2017. Speaking of the Russian-Iranian alliance, Putin said, "Russia and Iran share many years, if not centuries, of bilateral cooperation." He went on to say that "Iran and Russia have maintained diplomatic relations for more than 500 years."[6] Russia began delivering S-300 missile systems to Iran at the end of 2016, which Iran will use to defend its nuclear facilities from attack.

Douglas E. Schoen summarizes the ties between Russia and Iran:

What unites Russia and Iran today . . . are three common concerns: first, a shared goal of protecting Bashar al-Assad's regime in Syria, a mission that places them firmly against the United States and its Western allies; second, a common general interest in opposing radical Sunni Islamist movements, today exemplified by ISIS . . . and third, a common interest in smashing internal dissent in their own countries and quelling secessionist movements— whether from the Chechens in Russia or from the Kurds in Iran. Undergirding it all, however, is a common foe: the United States.[7]

History could soon give way to prophecy.

PERSIA—PRESENTLY AND PROPHETICALLY

No nation today is more dangerous than Iran—especially for Israel. Iran is the world's number-one sponsor of terror. Iran has spread its tentacles to other nations in its attempt to pave the way for the coming of its messiah, the Twelfth Imam. (More on this in a moment.) Iran's messianic ideology fuels its expansionist strategy. Through its own military and its surrogates, Iran now holds sway over five Arab nations: Lebanon, Yemen, the Palestinian territories, Syria, and Iraq. Iranian troops are just north of Israel in Syria. Iran's proxy Hezbollah in Lebanon is lying in wait on Israel's northern border, ready to strike at any time.

The term "Shiite crescent" was coined in 2004 by Jordan's King Abdullah. He noted that an Iranian-fueled "Shiite alliance was being formed from Tehran to Damascus and passing through Baghdad." Iran's sights are now set even higher. Iran's leaders speak not just of a "Shiite crescent" but of a "Shiite full moon."[8] Iran seeks a land corridor to the Mediterranean to anchor its territorial ambitions, allowing it to move people and supplies from Tehran to the sea.[9] The leader of the prominent Iran-supported Shiite group Asaib Ahl al-Haq says that "an alliance of Shiite forces across the region would be ready to achieve that goal by the time the hidden Shiite Imam Mahdi reappears." He adds that "the Shiite force will include the Islamic Revolution Guards Corps (I.R.G.C.) in Iran, the Lebanese Hezbollah, the Houthi movement in Yemen, the Popular Mobilization Forces (P.M.F) and other Shiite militant groups operating in Syria and Iraq."[10]

Time and again, Iran has taken advantage of chaos in nearby nations to promote its hegemonic agenda and ambitions. The success Iran has enjoyed in Iraq, Yemen, Lebanon, and Syria has emboldened its leaders. The *Guardian*'s Martin Chulov observes, "That should trouble every western leader and our regional allies because this will further embolden Iran to continue expanding, likely into the Gulf countries next, a goal they have explicitly and repeatedly articulated. Why should we expect them to stop if they've been at the casino, doubling their money over and over again, for a decade?"[11]

Middle East activist group Naame Shaam outlines Iran's support of its proxies in other nations:

- *Lebanon:* "From the 1980s to the beginning of the Arab Spring, Hezbollah received between $100m and $200m annually from Iran. Domestic economic decline and the increasing intervention in Syria led to this number . . . being cut to around $50m to $100m per year from 2010 onwards."

- *Iraq:* "From the 2003 invasion of Iraq until the end of Bush's presidency, Iran provided a range of Iraqi Shia militias with $10m to $35m a year, a number which skyrocketed after 2009 to $100m to $200m a year."
- *Palestine:* "From its consolidation of power in 2007 to the start of the Arab Spring in Syria and elsewhere in 2011, Hamas received approximately $100m to $250m per year from Iran. Hamas's refusal to back Assad led to a dramatic decline in funding."
- *Yemen:* "The Houthis have received anywhere between $10m and $25m a year since 2010."
- *Syria:* "Assad government forces and its allied militias received between $15bn and $25bn over the first five years of the conflict, amounting to between $3bn and $5bn per year."[12]

Despite Iran's strong influence in the region, commentator Alireza Nader writes, "One thing is clear: while Iran may appear to have the upper hand in Syria and perhaps the Middle East, Russia appears to be pulling the real strings."[13] This is exactly what we should anticipate if the Russian-led coalition of Ezekiel 38 is on the horizon.

Iran's game plan may be a "Shiite full moon" across the Middle East—a clear path to the Mediterranean—but Iran's main ambition is the destruction of the Jewish state. Israel fears Iran much more than it fears ISIS. Iran has a sophisticated military and a large army and is pursuing the nuclear prize. The Iran nuclear deal has temporarily frozen Iran's nuclear pursuits, yet the restrictions are only temporary. In exchange for placing a hold on its nuclear program, Iran received more than $100 billion to build up its military machine and support its surrogates.

Iran agreed to freeze its nuclear development in return for lifted sanctions, but these restrictions disappear after ten years. Moreover, there's always the risk of Iranian covert activity in the meantime. In violation of a UN resolution, Iran has an active ballistic missile program, which is useful for only one thing—delivering a nuclear payload. Iran is waiting but also working. The growing connection between North Korea and Iran is troubling.

The clock is ticking.

No nation has expressed its hatred of the Jewish state more vehemently and viciously than Iran. With rabid regularity, Iran calls for Israel's annihilation. If there's any doubt that Iran still despises Israel and wants to see Israel wiped off the face of the earth, their military hardware tells the tale:

Iran displayed various missile systems in a military parade in Tehran on Tuesday, many of which were emblazoned with slogans calling for the death of Israel. . . .

"Some of the trucks carrying weapons were adorned with banners showing a fist punching through a blue Star of David and the slogan 'Death

to Israel' in Persian," Agence France-Presse reported.
Another truck at the event had "Death to Israel"
emblazoned on its side in both Persian and Arabic, as
well as "Down with Israel" in English and an image
of the Israeli flag on fire.[14]

If this were not bad enough, Iran is propelled by its
"Twelver" brand of Shiite Islam, which focuses on the coming of the Twelfth Imam—Imam Muhammad al-Mahdi.
Twelvers believe that in the ninth century he disappeared in
the mosque of Samarra as a young boy without leaving any
descendants. They believe that since that time he has been
hidden by God—thus his alternate title "Hidden Imam." He's
also known as the Mahdi (Arabic for "rightly guided one").

For centuries Shiites have been waiting for the Mahdi
to emerge from hiding to bring global victory and usher in
an era of righteousness. Their eschatological view teaches
that the Mahdi will return near the end of the world. Joel
Rosenberg gives a helpful synopsis of the eschatological ideology that fuels Iran:

> Shias believe the Mahdi will return in the last days
> to establish righteousness, justice, and peace. When
> he comes, they say, the Mahdi will bring Jesus with
> him. Jesus will be a Muslim and will serve as his
> deputy, not as King of kings and Lord of lords as
> the Bible teaches, and he will force non-Muslims to
> choose between following the Mahdi or death. . . .

One thing that is fairly well agreed upon among devout "Twelvers" is that the Mahdi will end apostasy and purify corruption within Islam. He is expected to conquer the Arabian Peninsula, Jordan, Syria, "Palestine," Egypt and North Africa, and eventually the entire world. During this time, he and Jesus will kill between 60 and 80 percent of the world's population, specifically those who refuse to convert to Islam.[15]

Based on this ideology, and Iran's obsession with wiping out Israel, Rosenberg has rightly called Iran's mullah regime an "apocalyptic, genocidal death cult."[16]

Certainly Iran's Twelver ideology is a game changer. Iranian politics and aspirations cannot be divorced from this ideology. They believe the United States is the "Great Satan" and Israel is the "Little Satan."[17] Both are considered obstacles that need to be removed for the Mahdi's return. Added to all this, Twelvers believe it is their duty to hasten the Mahdi's coming, which they believe will occur in a time of chaos and turmoil. They believe they can put out the "welcome mat" for the Mahdi.

These views can be puzzling to Western minds, but even other Muslims are perplexed by Iran's ideology. The crown prince of Saudi Arabia expressed his inability to dialogue with Iran due to its belief in the coming of the Twelfth Imam:

The prince said that dialogue with Iran was impossible because of its belief in the Imam Mahdi,

the so-called hidden imam, who many Shiites
believe is a descendant of the Prophet Muhammad
who will return to save the world from destruction.
"Their stance is that the awaited Mahdi will come,
and they need to create a fertile environment for
the arrival of the awaited Mahdi, and they need to
take over the Islamic world," he said. "Where are the
common points that we might be able to reach an
understanding on with this regime?"[18]

If fellow Muslims can't reason with Iran due to its apocalyptic views, how can Israel or the West ever hope to reach
any common ground? Iran is driven by a dogma that seeks to
overrun the Islamic world—and annihilate Israel.

What we're witnessing in Iran strikingly sets the stage for
the events in Ezekiel 38–39.

LET'S TALK TURKEY

The Ottoman empire, centered in Turkey, lasted for more
than six hundred years and occupied the land of Israel for
four hundred years. In the wake of World War I, Mustafa
Kemal Atatürk founded the Republic of Turkey and served
as its first president from 1923 until his death in 1938. For
almost a hundred years, while dominated by Islam, Turkey
has remained a secular republic ruled by a parliament.

In the last decade, much has changed with the ascent of
President Recep Tayyip Erdoğan. He has dominated Turkish

politics since 2002. Erdoğan served as mayor of Istanbul (elected in 1994), as prime minister (beginning in 2003), and as president (since August 2014). Erdoğan towers over Turkey's political landscape. Since his rise to power, many have feared that he's an Islamist with ambition for greater power. Under Erdoğan, Turkey has been on the road to authoritarianism for several years. Years ago, Erdoğan likened democracy to "a train that you get off once you reach your destination."[19] We've learned a great deal recently about the destination he had in mind.

Erdoğan leveraged an attempted coup in July 2016 to purge the police force and military, strengthening his grip on the nation. Some have questioned whether the coup was secretly orchestrated by Erdoğan to justify his subsequent power grab. There's no way to know, but the result is the same: more power for the president.

A controversial referendum vote on April 16, 2017, narrowly passed (51.4 percent), giving sweeping new powers to President Erdoğan. The referendum promised to bring these (and other) changes:

- "Abolish the post of prime minister and transfer executive power to the president."
- "Allow the newly empowered president to issue decrees and appoint many judges and officials responsible for scrutinizing his decisions."
- "Limit the president to two five-year terms, but give the option of running for a third term if Parliament

truncates the second one by calling for early elections."

- "Allow the president to order disciplinary inquiries into any of Turkey's 3.5 million civil servants, according to an analysis by the head of the Turkish Bar Association."[20]

The referendum is a watershed event in Turkish history.

At the same time Erdoğan is grabbing power, Turkey's ties with Russia and Iran are strengthening, and relations between Turkey and Israel have taken a major turn for the worse.

Erdoğan's true colors are on full display when he talks about Jerusalem. His ultimate ambition to return Jerusalem to Muslim rule is clear. In a speech in Istanbul before millions who appeared to celebrate 562 years since the capture of Constantinople from European Christians, Erdoğan spoke these inflammatory words: "Conquest is Mecca, conquest is Saladin, it's to hoist the Islamic flag over Jerusalem again; conquest is the heritage of Mehmed II and conquest means forcing Turkey back on its feet."[21] Speaking of Jerusalem, Erdoğan said, "It's a symbol that unites us. All those who claim that Jerusalem is the Jew's holy city should be ashamed. We chose the name Saladin in order to send a message with the help of Allah that Jerusalem will always belong to the Kurds, to Turkey, to Arabs, to Muslims." As Erdoğan spoke, the IHH—an Islamist organization—marched in Istanbul "calling for the 'liberation of Jerusalem.'"[22]

On May 15, 2015, President Erdoğan spoke these chilling

words: "Unfortunately we the Muslims lost our aim to head towards Jerusalem. The water of our eyes froze, making us blind, and our hearts that were destined to beat for Jerusalem are now instead conditioned for rivalry, in a state of war with each other." In his analysis of this statement, commentator Burak Bekdil says, "In other words, Erdogan is calling the *ummah* [the Muslim community] to end its conflicts in order to unite behind a jihad march toward Jerusalem."[23]

About two years later, Erdoğan ratcheted up the rhetoric even further, delivering an anti-Semitic rant issuing a call for Muslims to swarm the Temple Mount in Jerusalem. The tirade "called on Muslims from around the world to flood the Al-Aqsa Mosque," which sits on the Temple Mount. He said, "Every day that Jerusalem is under occupation is an insult to Muslims."[24] He called on Muslims to "join forces to protect Jerusalem from Israel's Judaization attempts."[25]

Some believe Erdoğan considers himself a twenty-first-century Saladin, who, like the Muslim leader during the Crusades, will similarly rally the forces of Islam to reassert control over Israel and Jerusalem. Events in Turkey, accelerated by Erdoğan's emergence, are shifting suddenly and point toward the fulfillment of the invasion of Israel prophesied in Ezekiel 38.

WHAT DOES IT MEAN?

The war in Syria, the rise of ISIS, and at the same time a withdrawal, or at least a weakening, of US influence has sparked a Russian-Iranian-Turkish triumvirate that is gaining momentum. While the advance of this trio raises all kinds of geopolitical considerations that give Western leaders headaches, the prophetic implications are even more significant.

Writing almost forty years ago about world events in light of Bible prophecy, Charles Ryrie said,

> Turkey will move out of the orbit of Western influence and cooperation, and move into the sphere of Russian domination. What will trigger this, we do not know. But eventually Turkey will align herself with Russia and her other allies. It says the same for Iran, since Persia will also be a Russian ally in the coming war.[26]

How did Dr. Ryrie know these things back in 1981? Because he based his view on the Bible, not current events. With forty years of hindsight, we're now seeing what Ryrie knew was coming.

As all these developments converge, Israel sits at the epicenter of the region in the middle of the bull's-eye, just a few miles south of the Syrian war zone. What's happening seems to be part of the buildup for the fulfillment of biblical prophecy. Major tremors are moving the pieces into place.

The three-nation axis of Russia, Iran, and Turkey could quickly morph into the full coalition the prophet Ezekiel predicted long ago. In the increasingly volatile atmosphere in the world, not much would have to happen for these nations to conspire against Israel and challenge the West. We can all imagine a host of events that could trigger this offensive.

Time will tell whether the convergence of these three allies is part of the near trajectory that leads to the War of Gog and Magog or whether they're part of a longer orbit. Either way, as we'll see throughout this book, we can be sure that God is at work behind the scenes, ruling and overruling in the affairs of humanity.

CHAPTER 6

VLADIMIR PUTIN, RISING CZAR

IT'S PUTIN'S WORLD
HEADLINE IN THE *ATLANTIC*

PUTIN IS READY FOR WAR AND NOBODY ELSE IS.
DOUGLAS SCHOEN'S *PUTIN'S MASTER PLAN*

"Putin's Russia is clearly the biggest and most dangerous threat facing the world today."[1] So laments Russian chess grand master Garry Kasparov in his book *Winter Is Coming*.

He's right.

"Putinism" is mushrooming in Russia and spreading throughout the world. Putin rules over a neo-Czarist Russia. *Forbes* has named Vladimir Putin the world's most powerful person four years in a row, saying, "From the motherland to Syria to the U.S. presidential elections, Russia's leader continues to get what he wants."[2] In 2014 Vladimir Putin was chosen as Russia's "Man of the Year," the fifteenth time (in a row) he was given that honor.[3] Putin is the leading candidate for *Time* magazine's "Person of the Year" in 2017, as he was named in 2007.

Putin has fashioned what he calls a "vertical of power," which means "the entire structure of Russian political power rests on one man."[4] According to former Soviet leader Mikhail Gorbachev, Putin views himself as "second only to God."[5]

LORD OF THE RING

A bizarre story from June 2005 illustrates Putin's belief that he's a law unto himself and takes what he wants. Putin was hosting a group of businessmen in a palace in Petersburg, Russia, including Robert Kraft, owner of the New England Patriots, whose team had won the Super Bowl in February. When the meeting ended, the executives gathered around Putin to greet him and pose for photographs. It was all smiles. One of the executives asked Kraft, "Why don't you show the president your ring?" Kraft didn't normally wear his Super Bowl ring but kept it in his suit pocket. The ring was laced with 124 diamonds and engraved with Kraft's name (and valued at $25,000). Kraft fished the ring from his pocket and handed it to Putin, who put it on his finger and said, "I could kill somebody with this."

As the gathering broke up, Kraft held out his hand for the ring, but Putin put it in his pocket and abruptly left. Putin evidently assumed it was a gift, but Kraft was astonished by Putin's actions. Kraft appealed to the chairman of Citigroup, who helped arrange the meeting, and even to the White House. He was told it would be best to say it was intended as a gift. Kraft objected strenuously that it was not a gift. He was told repeatedly that it would be best if he gave the ring as a present. Kraft eventually acquiesced and four days later issued a public statement that the ring was a "symbol of the respect and admiration that I have for the Russian people and the leadership of President Putin."[6] Putin's actions gnawed at Kraft for years. "Kraft had another ring made, and the original went into the Kremlin library, where gifts to the head of state are collected."[7]

Few believe there was any misunderstanding. Putin stole the ring. His open, unapologetic theft of a Super Bowl ring is a microcosm of his brash, thuggish inclination to grab what he wants without fear. Whether a ring or a realm, Putin takes what he wants and gets away with it.

Putin's success in his raw expansionist aggression has emboldened him to keep moving forward. Putin invaded Georgia and "took Crimea with barely a shot fired. He flooded Eastern Ukraine with agents and weaponry."[8] When he annexed Crimea, protests in Russia against him stopped, and his personal approval ratings shot up from 60 percent to 80 percent. Putin seems to have a sense of invincibility and destiny. In September 2014, Putin boasted, "If I wanted, in two days I could have Russian troops not only in Kiev, but also in Riga, Vilnius, Tallinn, Warsaw and Bucharest."[9]

Putin knows that military power is key. In a Russian documentary in 2015, Putin said, "A well-known person once said, 'You can get much farther with a kind word and a Smith & Wesson than you can with just a kind word.'"[10] In keeping with that philosophy, he's arming Russia to the teeth.

While Western European nations are busy slashing military budgets, Russia is spending more than ever. Russian military spending increased 25.6 percent from 2014 to 2015, an increase of $20 billion in just one year. Since he took power in 2000, Putin has boosted military spending twentyfold.[11] Uniformed manpower has declined in every Western European nation since 2011, while Russian personnel increased 25 percent to more than 850,000. Putin's goal is one million combat-ready troops by 2020.[12]

Douglas Schoen, an influential Democratic campaign consultant, writes, "Over the next decade, Putin plans to acquire and develop four hundred new intercontinental ballistic missiles (ICBMs); more than two thousand next-generation tanks; six hundred modernized combat aircraft; eight nuclear ballistic submarines; fifty warships; . . . and about 17,000 new military vehicles."[13] Russia already has the world's largest nuclear arsenal but "added thirty-eight nuclear missiles in 2014 and another forty in 2015."[14] Russia's nuclear storehouse is staggering.

Putin wants military parity, if not superiority, to the United States, and the gap is closing. If Putin serves three full terms as president, as he's allowed by law, he can rule until 2024. He has many years left to achieve his goals. And who knows if he will relinquish power in 2024? If he does step down, he may simply hand the reins over to a puppet to serve on his behalf, as he did in 2008 with Dmitry Medvedev. Putin's grasp on Russia is strong, his reach immense, and his ambition boundless.

"A SENSE OF HIS SOUL"

When President George W. Bush met with Putin for the first time (in 2001), he said he "looked the man in the eye" and "was able to get a sense of his soul."[15] Bush has been chided, even mocked, for this remark, but he had the right idea. There's something in Putin's soul, as with every person, that drives him. What powers Putin?

Vladimir Vladimirovich Putin was born on October 7, 1952, in Leningrad. The city was still scarred by the German siege in World War II and languishing in deprivation and fear. Putin's father sustained injuries in the war that left him limping in pain the rest of his life. Putin grew up in cramped communal quarters, mesmerized by the power of the Soviet state. He fulfilled his dream in 1975, joining the KGB. Since that time, Putin has been a Soviet man.

The Soviet empire dissolved on December 25, 1991. Vladimir Putin has never gotten over it. The *New Yorker* article "Trump, Putin, and the New Cold War" captures the essence of Putin's humiliation over the fall of the Soviet Union and his drive to bring back the glory days:

> Putin's resentment of the West, and his
> corresponding ambition to establish an anti-Western
> conservatism, is rooted in his experience of decline
> and fall—not of Communist ideology, which was
> never a central concern of his generation, but, rather,
> of Russian power and pride. . . .

Posted [as a KGB agent] in one of the grayest of
the Soviet satellites [East Germany], Putin entirely
missed the sense of awakening and opportunity that
accompanied perestroika, and experienced only the
state's growing fecklessness. At the very moment the
Berlin Wall was breached, in November, 1989, he was
in the basement of a Soviet diplomatic compound in
Dresden feeding top-secret documents into a furnace.
As crowds of Germans threatened to break into the
building, officers called Moscow for assistance, but,
in Putin's words, "Moscow was silent." Putin returned
to Russia, where the sense of post-imperial decline
persisted. The West no longer feared Soviet power;
Eastern and Central Europe were beyond Moscow's
control; and the fifteen republics of the Soviet Union
were all going their own way. An empire shaped by
Catherine the Great and Joseph Stalin was dissolving.[16]

Fareed Zakaria adds,

To understand Putin, you have to understand Russia.
The last hundred years for that country have seen
the fall of the monarchy, the collapse of democracy,
the great depression, World War II with its tens
of millions of Russians dead, Stalin's totalitarian
brutalities, the collapse of communism, the breakup
of the Soviet Union, and Boris Yeltsin's years of chaos
and corruption.[17]

Many events have played a formative role in Putin's view of the world, but the collapse of the Soviet Union seems to have scarred and shaped him more than anything else. In 2005, in his annual state of the nation address to parliament, referring to the dissolution of the Soviet Union, he said, "First and foremost it is worth acknowledging that the demise of the Soviet Union was the greatest geopolitical catastrophe of the century."[18]

Putin is bent on rebuilding the Soviet Union and restoring the glory of imperial Russia. He wants Russia to regain lost territory and dominate the nations that brought about the Soviet dissolution. Part of restoring this greatness is securing allies. In his efforts to restore the greatness of mother Russia, Putin is tirelessly scouring the globe in search of willing allies. He's obsessed with elevating Russia's international influence.

Putin has spearheaded the formation of a Eurasian Economic Union (EAEU). The main goal is to merge the former Soviet republics into a unified economic and political confederation. Many believe this is Putin's attempt to restore the Soviet Union. Thus far, the union includes just five states: Armenia, Belarus, Kazakhstan, Kyrgyzstan, and Russia. Russia is trying to create an alternative and counterbalance to the European Union. Commentator Areg Galstyan writes, "In other words, Moscow is trying to institutionalize its influence in the Eurasian space, collecting fragments of the collapsed Soviet empire."[19] Once again, Putin's desire to restore the empire is his driving motivation.

Former Secretary of State Condoleezza Rice warns that "Russian President Vladimir Putin is trying to re-establish 'Russian greatness' with his assertiveness and aggressiveness abroad." She further cautions that this is a "dangerous time with the Russians."[20]

VLADIMIR PUTIN: KEY DATES[21]
1975—Joins the KGB.
1992—Departs the KGB.
1992–1994—Serves as deputy mayor of St. Petersburg.
1997–1998—Works in the administration of President Boris Yeltsin.
August 9–December 31, 1999—Serves as acting prime minister of Russia.
May 7, 2000—Inaugurated as second president of the Russian Federation.
May 7, 2004—Begins second term as president.
December 19, 2007—Named *Time* Person of the Year.
May 7, 2008—Not permitted to serve a third consecutive term; relinquishes power to his puppet Dmitry Medvedev. Medvedev is inaugurated as president and appoints Putin as his prime minister.
May 7, 2012—Begins his third term as president (presidential terms are now six years).
September 1, 2016–present—Accused of hacking and influencing US presidential elections and collusion with Donald Trump but denies any Russian involvement.

KREMLIN, INC.

During Putin's time in office, the lines between Russian oil interests and the Kremlin have been blurred to the point of no distinction. Affairs of state and business are fused. Where they diverge is difficult to discern. Putin has learned how to take advantage of privatized Russian assets to enrich himself. Putin's ties to business are so extensive, Russians sometimes refer to the Putin regime as "Kremlin, Inc." and call Putin the CEO.

Putin oversaw the dissolution of major Russian oil interests that have been sold to shadowy figures. Yukos Oil was dismantled and sold at an auction. The "auction" was all theatrics. Only one person put in a bid, and the entire auction lasted ten minutes. No one outside the Kremlin knew who purchased these interests, although Russian oligarchs certainly control them with Putin's hand in their pockets.[22] Since he assumed the presidency in 2000 (with a break from 2008 to 2012), Putin has raked in billions from business deals mainly within the energy sector.

Estimates of Putin's personal wealth vary wildly. According to official reports he owns a small apartment, a shared garage, and a few cars. His income in 2014 was reported as a modest 7.65 million rubles ($119,000). However, Putin has amassed a vast fortune, enriching himself and his close friends and allies. His palace on the Black Sea cost $1 billion. His net worth has been estimated at between $70 billion and $200 billion.[23] Putin may be the richest man in the world. Bill Gates is worth around $80 billion, so Putin is either close to the world's richest person or more than twice as rich.

The CEO of Kremlin, Inc., is doing quite well.

MAN WITH A PLAN

From the outside, Putin's actions may seem haphazard or disjointed. Much of the time he may seem like an "unpredictable tyrant, obsessed with power, violence, and conquest, who lashes out at neighboring countries impulsively and spasmodically."[24] But these characterizations are far off the mark. There's no doubt he possesses a clear vision of his objectives.

Douglas Schoen summarizes Putin's global master plan: "Putin is a calculating master of geopolitics with a master plan to divide Europe, destroy NATO, reestablish Russian influence in the world, and, most of all, marginalize the United States and the West in order to achieve regional hegemony and global power. And his plan is working."[25]

As you can see, Putin is not a wild-eyed tyrant. He has a specific plan.

The West faces a greater threat from Russia today than at any point during the Cold War. Douglas Schoen continues:

Vladimir Putin is many things—KGB officer, master politician, multibillionaire, ruthless autocrat—but, above all, Vladimir Putin is a man with a plan. His plan is to unmake the world order that has stood since the end of the Cold War, especially in Europe, and replace it with one where Russia has the power, influence, and military strength to get its way on any issue. This means subjugating Russia's immediate

neighbors and integrating them into a Russia-
centric political and economic system, neutralizing
Europe and ending the transatlantic relationship
with America, and seeding an endless series of global
crises that drain the West's ability and desire to
influence global affairs while promoting the interests
of Russia and its allies. In short, Putin plans to make
the twenty-first century the Russian century.[26]

At the same time Putin is implementing his master plan
by invading neighboring nations and building ties with Syria,
Iran, and Turkey, he's also employing a global strategy of all-
out cyber-warfare. Russian hackers have meddled in the 2016
US presidential election as well as elections in France and
Germany. They've compromised the US State Department,
the Pentagon, and the White House and have even gained
access to at least some of former president Barack Obama's
e-mails.[27] Grave concerns abound concerning Russian hacking of elections and the undermining of democracy. This is
another prong in Putin's global strategy to weaken the West.
All the energy the US press and Congress have expended on
Russia and Putin in the wake of the US presidential election are evidence that Putin's strategy has already worked,
at least to some degree. The cover of *Time* dated May 18,
2017, is a graphic depiction of the White House overtaken
by Russia. Inside that issue of *Time*, Massimo Calabressi
notes, "By raising doubts about the validity of the 2016 vote
and the vulnerability of future elections, Russia has achieved

its most important objective: undermining the credibility of American democracy."[28]

One thing is sure: Putin has a global strategy, and on all fronts, he seems to be getting what he wants.

THE MAIN QUESTION

In light of Putin's actions, many have speculated whether he could be the Russian leader known as Gog in Ezekiel 38–39. Speaking at churches and prophecy conferences, I've been asked this question many times. Is Putin the Russian leader that Ezekiel foretold—the one who will marshal an attack against Israel in the latter years?

While it's possible he *could* be, we must always avoid irresponsible attempts to identify any current world leader with an end-times figure. Many have fallen into this trap. Any form of date setting, identifying the Antichrist with a contemporary person, or pinpointing someone as Gog or as any other person mentioned in end-times prophecy must be soundly rejected.

Having said that, we sometimes see people from the past or present who demonstrate the same characteristics as end-times figures. The Bible foretold the rise of Seleucid ruler Antiochus Epiphanes, for example, and uses him as a type or prefigure of the final Antichrist (see Daniel 8). Other dictators from the past like Alexander the Great, Pharaoh, Nebuchadnezzar, Napoleon, Hitler, and Stalin serve as adumbrations of the final Antichrist.

Keeping this in mind, Putin is forging economic, political,

and military ties with the nations outlined in Ezekiel 38:1-6. He also possesses some of the traits (military aggression, pride, and greed) that Gog possesses. Joel Rosenberg gives his assessment about any connection between Putin and Gog:

> Over the years, people have asked me if Putin might be the Russian dictator referred to as "Gog" in the Biblical prophecies of "Gog and Magog" in Ezekiel 38–39. I suspect as Putin continues to re-emerge, those questions will begin to be asked again. Here's my quick answer: It's too soon to draw such a conclusion. There's much more that would have to happen to indicate that Putin was the "Gog" of Bible prophecy. But there's no question in my mind that Putin is *Gog-esque*. He is dangerous, and both Israel and the West should keep a close and wary eye on him, especially given all that Putin has done to build a strategic alliance between Russia and Iran and the other countries mentioned in the "Gog and Magog" prophecies.[29]

Time will tell. What we can say is that Putin can be neither definitively identified as Gog nor conclusively ruled out. He may be responsible for the invasion of Israel foretold in Ezekiel, or he may be setting the stage for another leader waiting in the wings. But at a minimum Putin is showing us a faint foreshadowing of what's coming. Make no mistake—Gog will come, but only in God's time.

Maybe very soon!

CHAPTER 7

RED DAWN: THE WAR OF GOG AND MAGOG

YOU AND ALL YOUR ALLIES–A VAST AND AWESOME ARMY–WILL ROLL DOWN ON THEM LIKE A STORM AND COVER THE LAND LIKE A CLOUD.

EZEKIEL 38:9

I grew up during the height of the Cold War in the 1960s and 1970s. The Soviet Union was the rival superpower to the United States. The Soviet hammer and sickle loomed large. Communism was the dark threat hanging over the world. At school we ran through drills preparing us to take cover in the event of a nuclear detonation nearby (although I always wondered what good it would do to get under my desk). Deep down, every American's worst nightmare was a nuclear exchange with the Soviets or a Russian invasion of our homeland. We prayed it would never happen but knew it was possible.

In 1984, a movie that tapped into this foreboding fear hit the big screen. *Red Dawn* instantly became a favorite for me and my friends. It became an overnight classic. The movie depicts a surprise Russian invasion of the United States set in a small town in Colorado.

Red Dawn opens with a gripping, surreal scene. A group of high school students are sitting in class when suddenly one student looks out the window and sees foreign paratroopers dropping from the sky. As the students struggle to make sense of what's happening, they begin to flee, and pandemonium breaks out. The plotline focuses on a group of teenagers who escape into the mountains and use guerilla tactics to disrupt their Russian and Cuban occupiers.

After the fall of the Soviet empire in 1991, and the end of the Cold War, fear of a "red dawn" receded into the history books . . . or did it?

Russia's rise has reawakened old fears—both at home and abroad. These concerns appear to be justifiable, especially in light of biblical prophecy. According to Scripture, the fictional surprise attack on the United States depicted in *Red Dawn* will someday become fact in the land of Israel when Russia and its allies spring a shocking surprise attack.

Russia's aggressive posture shows no signs of relaxing and is even tightening, and it could lead in the near future to the "red dawn" invasion of Israel predicted in Ezekiel 38–39. Since this war could be on the horizon, we need to understand what will happen and how events today could point toward its fulfillment. Referring to these chapters in Ezekiel, David Jeremiah says, "In these two chapters, God gave to Ezekiel the most detailed prophecy concerning war in the entire Bible."[1]

Let's examine some of those details.

THE RUSSIAN AIM

When Russia's forces invade the Holy Land, they will have four main motivations.

First, they desire to *steal* the Promised Land from Israel (see Ezekiel 38:12). Jewish presence in the land has been a global issue since 1948. A string of wars have been waged against Israel by its Muslim neighbors over the mere presence of the Jewish people in their ancient homeland. Added to that, the third most holy site in Islam, the Dome of the Rock and Al-Aqsa Mosque, sits on the Jewish Temple Mount in Jerusalem. Taking permanent possession of the Temple Mount in Jerusalem could be motivation for the Islamic invaders listed in Ezekiel 38. Prophecy expert Randall Price writes, "Orthodox Jews in the Temple movement in Israel generally agree that the war of Gog and Magog is to be the next of Israel's wars, and believe that it will be fought over possession of Jerusalem and the Temple Mount."[2] The presence of the massive Islamic contingent in the Russian coalition, and their desire to steal land, supports this idea.

Second, the invaders will come to *seize* the assets of Israel. What spoil or plunder will they seek? We can't say for sure, but recent discoveries of vast oil and gas reserves in the Golan Heights and Israel's coastal waters could figure into Russia's calculations. The Tamar and Leviathan fields are massive and virtually untapped. Currently, the world is experiencing an oil bonanza, but that could change quickly. Black gold could play a part in end-times events.

Third, driven by anti-Semitism, the Russian-led invaders will come to *slaughter* the Jewish people and wipe them off the face of the earth (see Ezekiel 38:10, 16). This is in keeping with the hatred of the Jewish people by their Muslim neighbors that we see today. They would love nothing more than to destroy the Jewish people and the Jewish state. They've attempted several times to bring this to pass. Russia also has a long, ugly history of anti-Semitism.

Fourth, the Russian assault force will attack to *scare* the West and *stifle* the influence of the Antichrist, the king of the west, who will be Israel's ally as a result of the treaty referenced in Daniel 9:27. In a bold power grab, the invasion of Israel will be considered an attack against Israel's ally and protector, the Western confederacy, attempting to test their mettle or even tempting them to launch a Middle East counterattack. The constant threats of Vladimir Putin against Europe and NATO are consistent with this strategy to intimidate and threaten the West.

The Russian leader will be driven by his own agenda, with a desire to *steal* the land of Israel, *seize* its assets, *slaughter* the Jewish people, and *stifle* the power of the West or suck them into a war in the Middle East.

Hooks in the Jaws

Ezekiel leaves no doubt that the Russian leader will come into Israel for his own nefarious reasons; however, Ezekiel doesn't want the human element to overshadow the sovereign plan of God. Ezekiel graphically depicts the Russian invasion as the result of God putting hooks in the jaws of the Russian leader and drawing him out. Ezekiel wants us to know above all else that God is in control of all that's happening. He is sovereign—even over evil. Nothing occurs outside his prophetic plan.

Over the years there's been speculation about what event God will use to hook the Russians and draw them into the land of Israel. The hooks could be Russia's alliances with Islamic nations like Iran that want to wipe Israel off the map. Randall Price says, "Russia could easily fulfill the role of Gog, for its current economic hardships and political instability have led Russia to forge military alliances with Islamic powers that continually call for Israel's destruction."[3]

Another possible scenario is that the Antichrist's move to forge or enforce a peace treaty with Israel and her neighbors will be interpreted as a threat to Russia's power and will precipitate a disastrous countermove by Russia and its Islamic allies.

Thomas Ice presents another possibility:

For over fifteen years I have speculated that the "hook in the jaw" of Gog that God could use to bring a reluctant Russia down upon the land of Israel could be some thing like the following scenario that I articulated to Hal Lindsey on a National television show in 1991 on the day the first Gulf War ended: I could see the Muslims approaching the Russians and telling them that America has set a precedent for an outside power coming into the Middle East to right a perceived wrong. (America has done it again in recent years by going into Afghanistan and Iraq.) On that basis, Russia should help her Muslim friends by leading them in an overwhelming invasion of Israel in order to solve the Middle East Conflict in favor of the Islamic nations. Will this be the "hook in the Jaw" of Gog? Only time will tell. But something is up in the Middle East and Russia appears to have her fingerprints all over things.[4]

There will be many twists and turns in the days ahead, but Russia's increased involvement in the Middle East will certainly play a key role in pulling them into invading Israel. Whatever the hooks in the jaws may be, Russia will fulfill this prophecy according to God's sovereign will and on his timetable.

THE RUSSIAN ANNIHILATION

When the Russian-led horde descends on Israel, it will look like Israel is finished. Surprised and surrounded, the Israelites will be seized by unimaginable panic. Nothing in Israel's modern history will compare. Not the Six-Day War in 1967. Not the Yom Kippur War in 1973. Yet in a stunning reversal of fortunes, the invincible invaders who come to possess the mountains of Israel will perish on those same mountains. God will come down to rescue his people. Almighty God will intervene to win the battle. Those who come to loot Israel will themselves be looted by Israel.

Ezekiel 38–39 describes an overwhelming, sudden destruction when the forces of Gog meet God. What looks like a massive mismatch between Russia and Israel now becomes an infinitely greater mismatch as Gog faces the living God. Here's how Ezekiel graphically describes the bloodbath:

> This is what the Sovereign LORD says: When Gog invades the land of Israel, my fury will boil over! In my jealousy and blazing anger, I promise a mighty shaking in the land of Israel on that day. All living things—the fish in the sea, the birds of the sky, the animals of the field, the small animals that scurry along the ground, and all the people on earth—will quake in terror at my presence. Mountains will be thrown down; cliffs will crumble; walls will fall to the earth. I will summon the sword against you on all the hills of Israel, says the Sovereign LORD. Your men will turn their swords against each other. I will punish you and your armies with disease and bloodshed; I will send torrential rain, hailstones, fire, and burning sulfur!
>
> EZEKIEL 38:18-22

God will rise up in his fury to annihilate the invaders, employing four catastrophes to totally destroy Russia and its Islamic allies:

- *Shaking—a great earthquake (verses 19-20).* God will use a massive tremor with its epicenter in Israel to spread fear and confusion throughout the ranks of the Russian military machine. God will defeat and disorient the invading forces.
- *Slaughter—infighting among the troops of the various nations (verse 21).* In the chaos of the battle and the shaking of the earth under their feet, the Russian forces and their allies will turn against each other, resulting in a massive body count by friendly fire. Charles Dyer pictures the scene: "In the pandemonium, communication between the invading armies will break down and they will begin attacking each other. Every man's sword will be against his brother. Fear and panic will sweep through the forces so each army will shoot indiscriminately at the others."[5] God will repeat what he did on previous occasions in the Old Testament to deliver his people, turning the enemies upon themselves (see Judges 7:22; 1 Samuel 14:20; 2 Chronicles 20:22-25).
- *Sickness—disease and plagues (verse 22a).* The ruin of the invaders will be accelerated by additional supernatural disasters. God will unleash a lethal epidemic, adding to the misery and devastation already inflicted.
- *Storms—torrential rain, hailstones, fire, and burning sulfur/brimstone (verse 22b).* Reminiscent of Sodom and Gomorrah, God will rain fiery destruction from

on high on the invading army. There will be no place to hide. "The rain will combine with dirt and debris from the earthquake to produce massive mud slides and floods. Large hailstones will pelt the survivors, killing many. The 'burning sulphur' might be volcanic ash."[6]

Old Testament scholar Walter Kaiser summarizes the results of this war:

> Things will not end well for the nations that press their attack against Israel, for in the end, what they are doing is nothing less than an attack on God and his plan for time and eternity. In one great push, an axis of nations from that part of the world will make one huge incursion into the land of Israel, but that will call for the response of God himself. The carnage, bloodshed, and loss of life and power will be unrivaled up to that point in history. This will be at once one of the darkest, and yet also one of the brightest, days of all history, as God settles the issue in a startling way. Such is the predicted fortunes of the War of Gog and Magog against Israel in the end of the days of history's ongoing time line.[7]

The King James Version of Ezekiel 39:2 says, "I will turn thee back, and leave but the sixth part of thee," which indicates one-sixth of the invading army will be left alive. There's uncertainty about the meaning of the second Hebrew verb in

Ezekiel 39:2. This is the only time this verb is found in the Hebrew Bible. Some believe it was derived from the Hebrew *shisha*, which means "to leave a sixth part."[8] According to this understanding, only one in six (or around 17 percent) of the invading army will remain alive. But I prefer the reading that the entire invading army will be destroyed.[9] Most modern translations, including the New King James Version, omit any reference to the sixth part surviving and translate the verb as "to lead" or "to drive" (as in the New Living Translation: "I will turn you around and drive you toward the mountains of Israel").

Ezekiel 39:4 reveals the utter destruction of the invading army: "You and your army and your allies will all die on the mountains. I will feed you to the vultures and wild animals." If the destruction of the armies in the land of Israel were not bad enough, according to verse 6, there's another devastating dimension to the Russian invasion: "I will rain down fire on Magog and on all your allies who live safely on the coasts. Then they will know that I am the LORD." As we've seen, Magog includes territory in Russia as well as the nations of Central Asia, so not only will the invading forces be wiped out in Israel, but the Russian homeland will also suffer catastrophic collateral damage. God will wreak havoc by unleashing fire. The "fire" probably refers to devastation and military destruction (see Ezekiel 30:8, 14, 16). The "coasts" refers to "the farthest reaches of the known world," which certainly fits a description of the Russian motherland.[10] The raining of brimstone will inflict heavy casualties in the nation itself. The devastation will be so widespread, it "will cause Russia to cease being a political force in world affairs."[11]

The War of Gog and Magog in Islam

The Koran mentions Gog and Magog twice, calling them Yajuj and Majuj (18:96; 21:94). In Islam, there are ten major signs that portend the end of the age and the final resurrection. As with Christian eschatology, there are different opinions about the sequence of these signs, but the War of Gog and Magog is often the number four sign that the end is near.

The Islamic identity of Gog and Magog is quite strange. Muslims believe they are two groups of evil Turks who spread corruption through the earth during the days of Abraham. In order to restrain their evil, they were quarantined behind a great barrier. For centuries they have been trying to escape their prison. Finally, when the time is right, Allah will act, and the barrier will crumble, unleashing Gog and Magog. The horde will flood into the land of Israel to attack the Muslims residing there. According to Islamic teaching, Jesus will pray against Gog and Magog, and Allah will destroy them by sending a fatal plague.[12] The disease is depicted as either deadly boils or a malady that consumes the flesh from their bones.

Of course, this sounds very similar to the account in Ezekiel 38, except the players are different. Muhammad, who wrote the Koran more than one thousand years after Ezekiel prophesied, adapted and distorted this prophecy to fit his worldview. However, in a twist of prophetic irony, the prophecy of Gog and Magog will not be fulfilled by Allah on behalf of Muslims living in Israel but by the true God against the army (composed of Russians and Muslims) that will invade the Holy Land in the last days.

THE RUSSIAN AFTERMATH

In the wake of the stunning supernatural decimation of the invading army, Ezekiel tells us four things that will happen in Ezekiel 39:9-24.

Burning of the Weapons

Ezekiel 39:9-10 describes the fate of the weaponry that will be strewn throughout the land:

> Then the people in the towns of Israel will go out and pick up your small and large shields, bows and arrows, javelins and spears, and they will use them for fuel. There will be enough to last them seven years! They won't need to cut wood from the fields or forests, for these weapons will give them all the fuel they need. They will plunder those who planned to plunder them, and they will rob those who planned to rob them, says the Sovereign LORD.

Think of all the small arms, artillery, and so on that will be present after the invaders are wiped out. To finish burning all these weapons will take seven years! Are these weapons literal spears, clubs, and bows, or are they representative of their modern counterparts? We will discuss the meaning of the weapons listed in Ezekiel 39 in the next chapter. Either way, the weapons will be incinerated.

Burying of the Dead

The brash, bold offensive against Israel to steal land will result in the possession of only one piece of real estate for the invaders—their burial plots:

> I will make a vast graveyard for Gog and his hordes in the Valley of the Travelers, east of the Dead Sea. It will block the way of those who travel there, and they will change the name of the place to the Valley of Gog's Hordes. It will take seven months for the people of Israel to bury the bodies and cleanse the land. Everyone in Israel will help, for it will be a glorious victory for Israel when I demonstrate my glory on that day, says the Sovereign LORD.
>
> After seven months, teams of men will be appointed to search the land for skeletons to bury, so the land will be made clean again. Whenever bones are found, a marker will be set up so the burial crews will take them to be buried in the Valley of Gog's Hordes. (There will be a town there named Hamonah, which means "horde.") And so the land will finally be cleansed.
>
> EZEKIEL 39:11-16

The bodies will be so numerous that they will block the normal travel routes. The Russian-Iranian axis will set out to bury Israel, but God will bury the invaders instead. Seven months will be required to cleanse the land of all the dead bodies.

Banqueting of the Birds and Beasts

The gory, grisly result of the battle is described in Ezekiel 39:17-20:

> Now, son of man, this is what the Sovereign Lord says: Call all the birds and wild animals. Say to them: Gather together for my great sacrificial feast. Come from far and near to the mountains of Israel, and there eat flesh and drink blood! Eat the flesh of mighty men and drink the blood of princes as though they were rams, lambs, goats, and bulls—all fattened animals from Bashan! Gorge yourselves with flesh until you are glutted; drink blood until you are drunk. This is the sacrificial feast I have prepared for you. Feast at my banquet table—feast on horses and charioteers, on mighty men and all kinds of valiant warriors, says the Sovereign Lord.

God calls the gathering of the birds and the beasts to feed upon the carnage a "sacrificial feast." "Usually people slaughtered and ate sacrificed animals. Here, however, the men of Gog's armies will be sacrifices; they will be eaten by animals."[13] A similar scene will follow the final great campaign of Armageddon in Revelation 19:17-18.

Blessing of Salvation

The final result of the War of Gog and Magog will be a great spiritual awakening. In the book of Ezekiel the phrase "that you may know I am the LORD" or its equivalent occurs more than sixty times. This phrase recurs again and again in Ezekiel 38–39: "I will demonstrate my glory to the nations. Everyone will see the punishment I have inflicted on them and the power of my fist when I strike. And from that time on the people of Israel will know that I am the LORD their God" (Ezekiel 39:21-22; see also Ezekiel 38:16, 23; 39:6).

God will use the demonstration of his power and might to show the world who he really is. Many will shake it off and go on in their wicked ways. But many other Jews and Gentiles will turn to the Lord, acknowledging his power. Even in the dark days of the Great Tribulation, our merciful God will still be seeking and saving the lost, bringing about great spiritual revival.

Only God can save Israel then; only God can save us now.

CONCLUSION

There are five points to take away regarding the War of Gog and Magog:

1. The Gog-Magog War against Israel will be a

Russian-Islamic axis of nations bent on wiping Israel off the face of the earth. Specifically, they will come to *steal* land, *seize* spoil, *slaughter* the Jews, and *stifle* the Antichrist's growing power.

2. God will dramatically intervene, routing the invaders in a devastating defeat of a magnitude never seen in military history. Even Russia's homeland and headquarters will face devastating destruction.

3. The war will radically reorder world power. Here are a few of the more important ways this war will shape prophetic events:

It will *cripple* Islamic influence in the Middle East. Many Muslims live outside the Middle East, even the most populous nations such as Indonesia, but the annihilation of armies from Iran, Turkey, Central Asia, Libya, Sudan, and probably the near nations around Israel will deal a debilitating blow to Muslim power, effectively neutralizing this power bloc.

It will *crush* Russian aggression. The end-times king of the north will fall, never to rise again.

It will *create* a giant power vacuum. With the Russian-Islamic coalition taken out, the Western leader, whom we know as the Antichrist, will catapult onto the world scene. I've often wondered if the Antichrist might take credit for the destruction of the Russian horde, claiming possession of some secret weapon that enabled him to wipe them out. However events unfold, we know that by the middle of the Tribulation, the Antichrist will seize control of the world economically and politically (see Revelation 13). The destruction of the Russian-Islamic coalition will propel Antichrist's rise to global domination.

4. Through this victory, God will demonstrate his greatness and holiness to such an extent that all nations will be forced to acknowledge he alone is King of kings and Lord of lords. God will use this war to bring many Gentiles to faith in himself.

5. Likewise, the nation of Israel will come to a turning point, recognizing there is no one like the Lord their God.[14] The ultimate result of this war will be the national repentance and restoration of the Jewish people under the reign of their Messiah in the Kingdom.

We can learn many lessons for our lives today from the War of Gog and Magog, but two stand out: God is sovereign. And God is our only Savior.

Nothing is more important for us to hold on to than these two truths.

CHAPTER 8

HOW CLOSE ARE WE?

THE BOOK OF EZEKIEL PREDICTS THAT A LARGE FORCE, IDENTIFIED AS "MAGOG,"
FROM THE NORTH OF ISRAEL WILL ATTACK THE NATION. . . . THERE IS A LOT GOING
ON IN OUR CURRENT HEADLINES THAT LEADS ME TO BELIEVE IT COULD HAPPEN AT
ANY TIME. AND WHEN IT DOES, IT WILL TRANSPIRE IN RAPID SUCCESSION,
LIKE DOMINOES CLOSELY STACKED TOGETHER.

GREG LAURIE

The Russian bear continues to flex its muscle against its neighbors and in the Middle East. The Bear's footprint is expanding with a swelling presence in Syria, an increasing alliance with Iran, and strengthening ties with Turkey. As we've seen, all of this is headed toward a colossal conflict in the Holy Land led by Russia. One of the principal questions concerning this coming Middle East war is, When will it occur? How much longer until the first great war of the end times breaks out? Ezekiel 38 sheds light on the all-important timing question:

> Get ready; be prepared! Keep all the armies around
> you mobilized, and take command of them. A long
> time from now you will be called into action. In the

distant future you will swoop down on the land of
Israel, which will be enjoying peace after recovering
from war [NASB, "the sword"] and after its people
have returned from many lands to the mountains of
Israel. You and all your allies—a vast and awesome
army—will roll down on them like a storm and
cover the land like a cloud.

This is what the Sovereign LORD says: At that
time evil thoughts will come to your mind, and you
will devise a wicked scheme. You will say, "Israel is
an unprotected land filled with unwalled villages! I
will march against her and destroy these people who
live in such confidence!" . . .

Therefore, son of man, prophesy against Gog.
Give him this message from the Sovereign LORD:
When my people are living in peace in their land,
then you will rouse yourself. You will come from your
homeland in the distant north with your vast cavalry
and your mighty army, and you will attack my people
Israel, covering their land like a cloud. At that time in
the distant future, I will bring you against my land as
everyone watches, and my holiness will be displayed
by what happens to you, Gog. Then all the nations
will know that I am the LORD.

EZEKIEL 38:7-11, 14-16

The mention of swords and cavalry in Ezekiel 38 has led some
commentators to conclude that this battle occurred sometime

in the distant past. The weapons mentioned in Ezekiel chapters 38 and 39 are ancient weapons made out of wood such as bows, arrows, shields, war clubs, and spears (see 39:9). The means of transportation is horses (see 38:15). So how do we account for these ancient weapons if this invasion is in the end times? There are two plausible solutions to this problem.

First, it could be that by the time this event is fulfilled, nations will have reverted to archaic weapons and means of transportation due to oil shortages and other wars that have depleted these nations' resources, or possibly there will be some comprehensive disarmament treaties. Albert Einstein reportedly said, "I know not with what weapons World War III will be fought, but World War IV will be fought with sticks and stones." He could be right. John Walvoord favors this view of Ezekiel 38:

> [One possible] solution is that the battle is preceded
> by a disarmament agreement between nations. If
> this were the case, it would be necessary to resort
> to primitive weapons easily and secretly made if a
> surprise attack were to be achieved. This would allow
> a literal interpretation of this passage. . . . Whatever
> the explanation, the most sensible interpretation is
> that the passage refers to actual weapons pressed into
> use because of the peculiar circumstances of that day.[1]

A second interpretation is that Ezekiel spoke, inspired by the Holy Spirit, in language that the people of his day could understand. If he had spoken of planes, missiles, tanks, and rifles, this text would have been nonsensical to everyone until the twentieth century. As Paul Enns notes, "It is not necessary to suggest the final battle will be fought with horses. How would Ezekiel describe future warfare? Since he had no terminology for modern warfare, he would use the terminology of his time—horses and swords."[2] Walter Kaiser notes, "No doubt, we must understand here perhaps the modern equivalent for the use of horses, such as tanks and the like, for they would otherwise have had no meaning to those of Ezekiel's day. There is, however, the possibility that weather conditions and strategic reasons may force the use of horses where mechanized equipment would be impossible."[3]

Either way, the main point of Ezekiel's great prophecy is that a specific group of nations will attack Israel intent on completely destroying it. The emphasis is not on the specific weapons that will be used by these invaders. The point Ezekiel is making is that the invaders will wield weapons of destruction and that there will be all-out warfare. Understanding the weapons in light of their modern counterparts is not symbolic interpretation but rather situating God's Word in its historical context as understood by the original audience. The Holy Spirit speaks to people in their own context and culture in ways that communicate God's truth meaningfully and understandably.

Accounting for all the details of Ezekiel 38 and 39 leads to the conclusion that these chapters cannot have been fulfilled at any point in the past. No invasion of Israel even remotely similar to Ezekiel 38 has ever occurred in Israel's history, despite the claims of some who place the fulfillment of all or most biblical prophecy in the past.[4] John Walvoord states the issue accurately and succinctly: "There has never been a war with Israel which fulfills the prophecies of Ezekiel 38–39."[5]

Orthodox Jews view these chapters as a future event, referring to Ezekiel 38–39 as the "Wars of Gog" and seeing them as a series of three future invasions that will be the next of Israel's wars before the Messiah's appearance.[6] Eminent biblical scholar F. F. Bruce believes the events of Ezekiel 38–39 are located in the end times: "In Ezekiel 38:16 Gog's invasion of the land of Israel is to take place 'in the latter days'; here the original intention is eschatological."[7]

The War of Gog and Magog will occur in the end of days. That much seems clear. But is it possible to narrow the time frame down more specifically? What hints do we have in Ezekiel chapters 38 and 39 about the specific timing of this invasion? Numerous opinions have been offered by capable Bible scholars on this point, and every view is beset with weaknesses. The invasion has been placed at almost every key point in the end times. Let's look carefully at Ezekiel 38 and see if we can unravel some of the mystery.

IT'S ABOUT TIME

A group of authors and prophecy teachers place the Ezekiel invasion before the rapture of believers to heaven (this is the view depicted in the fictional Left Behind series); others believe it will occur between the time of the Rapture and the beginning of the seven-year Tribulation; others maintain it will transpire during the first half of the Great Tribulation; others believe it will take place in connection with the Battle of Armageddon at the end of the Great Tribulation. Many place it at the end of the Millennium, since there is a reference to Gog and Magog in Revelation 20:8. Others maintain that it will unfold in phases over the entire period of the Tribulation.[8] As you can see, this is among the most debated issues concerning the coming Russian invasion.

FOUR MAIN VIEWS OF THE TIMING OF THE RUSSIAN INVASION
Before the Rapture (or between the Rapture and the beginning of the Tribulation)
First half of the Tribulation (some put it close to the midpoint)
End of the Tribulation (equates Ezekiel 38–39 with Armageddon)
End of the Millennium (parallel with Revelation 20:8)

To simplify the process, we can reduce the scope of the problem by considering the textual hints or internal markers within Ezekiel 38 and the surrounding context that suggest when this battle will take place.[9] There are four chronological keys that narrow down the time when the events in Ezekiel 38–39 will come to pass.

The Placement

The most general clue rises from the broader context of Ezekiel's prophecy. The battle in Ezekiel 38–39 is placed between the regathering of Israel in Ezekiel 37 and the restoration of the Jewish people as they worship in the millennial Temple in Ezekiel 40–48. In Ezekiel 37 the Jewish people are regathered to the land *physically*, while in Ezekiel 40–48 they are restored to the Lord *spiritually* in the millennial kingdom. Ezekiel 38–39 falls between these two events.

Ezekiel 37	Ezekiel 38–39	Ezekiel 40–48
Jewish people regathered	War of Gog and Magog	Jewish people restored to the land physically, Lord spiritually

The regathering of the Jewish people to their land before this invasion is essential because, obviously, the Jewish people cannot be invaded if they aren't in their land.

As John Phillips notes, "The prophet put it between a discussion of the physical rebirth of the nation of Israel (chap. 37) and a long description of Israel's spiritual rebirth (chaps. 40–48). In other words, Russia's brief day of triumph lies somewhere between those two crucial events. . . . The prophet deliberately sandwiched Russia's 'date with destiny' between Israel's political and spiritual rebirths."[10]

This narrows the time frame for the Ezekiel 38 invasion down to the period between 1948, the year of the birth of the modern state of Israel, and the beginning of the thousand-year reign of Christ. We're now about seventy years after Israel's rebirth. Currently more than six million of the world's fourteen million Jews reside in Israel. This piece of the end-times puzzle is firmly in place.

The Prosperity

At the time this invasion occurs, Israel not only will be back in their land, but they also will be prosperous and thriving: "See, I care about you, and I will pay attention to you. Your ground will be plowed and your crops planted. I will greatly increase the population of Israel, and the ruined cities will be rebuilt and filled with people. I will increase not only the people, but also your animals. O mountains of Israel, I will bring people to live on you once again. I will make you even more prosperous than you were before" (Ezekiel 36:9-11). Russia and her allies will be lured into Israel to seize the nation's great wealth, indicating that Israel will be thriving in the latter years. Russia will come to Israel to "capture vast amounts of plunder, for the people are rich with livestock and other possessions now" (Ezekiel 38:12).

Massive gas reserves have been discovered in Israel in recent years, the most impressive being the Leviathan field, which contains around 20 trillion cubic feet of gas. This is a stunning economic game changer for Israel. Other gas reserves such as the Tamar field are so plentiful that they will meet Israel's needs for the next twenty-five years, leaving the Leviathan reserves available for export.

In May 2013, Secretary of State John Kerry told reporters, "I think there is an opportunity [for peace], but for many reasons it's not on the tips of everyone's tongue. People in

Israel aren't waking up every day and wondering if tomorrow there will be peace because there is a sense of security and a sense of accomplishment and of prosperity."[11] Kerry's statement, as well as leading economic indicators, shows that the second prerequisite for this invasion is in place.

The Period

Another chronological indicator is found in the phrases "latter years" (Ezekiel 38:8, NASB) and "last days" (38:16, NASB; NLT, "distant future" in both instances). We need to make a distinction between the last days for Israel in the Old Testament and the last days for the church in the New Testament. The "last days" in the New Testament refers to the last days of the church, which is the entire age between the two comings of Christ (see Hebrews 1:1-2). We currently live in the last days of the church.

"Last days" or "latter years" in the Old Testament refers to the last days for Israel, which are the seven years of Tribulation, culminating with the second coming of Christ and the setting up of his Kingdom on earth (see Deuteronomy 4:30; Isaiah 2:2; Jeremiah 30:24; Ezekiel 38:8, 16; Micah 4:1).

The reference to the "latter years" and "last days" in Ezekiel 38 eliminates any past fulfillment for these events. This could also render any time before the Tribulation unlikely, depending on how loosely one interprets the last days for Israel. I believe the Tribulation begins the "latter years" for Israel, but others are more expansive in their view of Israel's last days and believe this invasion could occur at any time. Either view is possible. If we're currently in the last days for Israel, this condition has also been met.

The Peace

Three times Ezekiel tells us that Russia will swoop into Israel when the people are dwelling securely and are at rest (see Ezekiel 38:8, 11, 14). Israel will be a "land filled with unwalled villages" when the surprise attack is launched (38:11). In ancient language this speaks of peace and safety, with little concern for protective measures.

There are not many occasions in God's prophetic program when Israel is secure and at rest. The Jewish people have been scattered and persecuted over the face of the earth, and not even in the future will Israel have many periods of rest and security.

Some believe this state of affairs is present in Israel today, so this condition could be fulfilled. We'll look at this issue as we briefly survey the four basic views of when the Russian invasion will transpire.

VIEW #1—EZEKIEL 38-39 IS THE SAME AS REVELATION 20:8

The simplest view for many scholars is to equate the only two biblical references to Gog and Magog in the Bible, found in Ezekiel 38 and Revelation 20. While this view is attractive in connecting the biblical dots, the different settings for these two passages to me eliminates this view from serious consideration.

	Gog and Magog in Ezekiel 38	Gog and Magog in Revelation 20:8
The Period	Before or during the Tribulation	After Christ's thousand-year reign (Revelation 20:1-6)
The Participants	Specific list of nations	Worldwide enemies of Christ

The only things these battles have in common are the terms *Gog* and *Magog* and the total annihilation of the enemy.[12] But if we view these two events as distinct, the question arises—how do we explain the identical names used for them? One common explanation is that the apostle John was simply using "Gog and Magog" as a kind of shorthand, the way we might use "Waterloo" to describe the final battle in Revelation 20. Rather than giving all the details of what will happen, John employs a well-known biblical allusion to communicate that nations will invade Israel and be wiped out by God just like what is described in Ezekiel 38–39. John is telling us in the briefest way possible that this will be another Gog and Magog, even though the two events are separated by more than a thousand years. In the same way that we speak of World War I and World War II, this will be Gog and Magog I and Gog and Magog II.

VIEW #2—THE WAR CAN HAPPEN AT ANY TIME

An impressive array of scholars and commentators believe all the preconditions for the fulfillment of Ezekiel 38–39 are currently in place, including Israel's prosperity and security. For them, this war can happen at any time. Walter Kaiser believes the Russian-led invasion of Israel will occur before the Tribulation begins. "It appears that before the final seven years begin, a Russian-Iranian confederation along with most Arab states will decide to act against Israel in the Gog-Magog plot."[13] Randall Price favors this view: "There is nothing in the description of Israel in Ezekiel 38–39 that does not fit the reality of the modern State of Israel today."[14]

Joel Rosenberg believes conditions in Israel today are ripe for this invasion to occur at any time: "The point here is that never before in her modern history has Israel been so secure, so prosperous, so eager to give up land for peace."[15] He adds,

> For the first time since the book of Ezekiel was written more than 2,500 years ago, it is now possible that the two prerequisites of relative peace and rising prosperity in Israel are already checked off God's to-do list, and that the rest of the prophecies will soon come true as well.
>
> Israel has been reborn as a country. Millions of Jews have poured back into the Holy Land. The deserts have bloomed. The economy is booming. The ancient ruins are being rebuilt. Israel has signed peace treaties, truces, cease-fire agreements, and/or other diplomatic and economic accords with all of its immediate neighbors. It has all happened just as

Ezekiel told us it would happen, and all of it begs the question: What will happen next?[16]

Those who hold this view believe that the War of Gog and Magog will happen before the Tribulation, thus eliminating the Islamic threat and allowing the Jewish people to rebuild the Temple in Jerusalem as required by Scripture (see Matthew 24:15; 2 Thessalonians 2:4).

Others are quick to point out that Israel today, while secure in one sense, is far from what is described in Ezekiel 38. David Jeremiah says,

This is clearly one condition that has not yet occurred. There has never been a time in Israel's existence, ancient or modern, when it has not been concerned about defense. Israel has always been surrounded by enemies. Even today Israel is constantly threatened from all sides by extremely hostile neighbors many times its size. It has already fought three major wars in its brief modern history, and Israel's close neighbor Iran is rabidly eager to annihilate it.

There is no country on earth as massively armed for its size and as constantly vigilant as Israel. Every young Israeli man is required to undergo three years of military training, and every young woman trains for two years. Visit Israel today and you will see its readiness for war on display everywhere. Armed soldiers are stationed in every strategic location, and security is the highest priority. One cannot enter a shop or restaurant without going through a metal detector. No, Israel is not at peace or anywhere close to it.[17]

Israel today is an armed camp, living under a tenuous truce with only two of its Arab neighbors—Egypt and Jordan—and both of those agreements could be in dire jeopardy with current events in the Middle East. The rest of its neighbors would love nothing more than to drive every Israelite into the Mediterranean Sea if they could. The reason they do not is because Israel possesses a formidable military machine that is more than a match for its neighbors.

To me, the prerequisite for peace does not seem to be fully in place, but it could be soon.[18]

VIEW #3—THE WAR IN EZEKIEL 38-39 IS THE SAME AS THE CAMPAIGN OF ARMAGEDDON

This view equates Ezekiel 38–39 with Revelation 19:11-21. One point in favor of this view is that both of these battles are great end-times conflagrations in the land of Israel, and both mention the birds feeding on the carnage (see Ezekiel 39:17-19; Revelation 19:17-18). While there are undoubtedly some similarities between the two passages, here are a few of the significant differences between these two events that demonstrate they are two separate end-times wars:

Gog and Magog	Armageddon
Leader is Gog	Leader is Antichrist
Israel is at rest/living securely	No mention of Israel's security
Specific nations: Russian-Islamic coalition	All nations
Nations know that the Lord is God	Nations are destroyed

Additionally, at the end of the Great Tribulation, Israel will not be at rest and living securely as Ezekiel 38 requires. The Jewish people will be scattered and pursued by the Antichrist (see Revelation 12:13-17). Therefore, the invasion described by Ezekiel could not be a part of the Battle of Armageddon at the end of the Great Tribulation.

VIEW #4—THE WAR WILL TRANSPIRE DURING THE FIRST HALF OF THE TRIBULATION

While I hold open the possibility that view #2 might be correct, I favor placing this invasion in the first half of the coming Tribulation because it best explains the security requirement. I don't believe what we see in Israel today meshes with the description of rest and security in Ezekiel 38. However, Scripture tells us the day is coming when Israel will be secure and at rest. So how will this come about? Charles Dyer and Mark Tobey suggest, "Perhaps a treaty [will be] forged by an outside power that is strong enough to enforce the treaty's conditions and compromises."[19] The prophet Daniel tells us how this peace will come to pass: "The ruler [the Antichrist] will make a treaty with the people for a period of one set of seven [years]" (Daniel 9:27).

Daniel reveals that in the end times, a group of ten leaders will spearhead a coalition of countries that will reunite the Roman empire (the Western confederacy). Out of this Group of Ten, which I call the G-10, a strong man will rise to power. He is the final Antichrist, who will take control of the G-10. This regional leader will emerge on the world stage as a peacemaker, accomplishing what no one else has been able to do—crafting a seven-year treaty of protection and peace with the people of Israel that will solve the Middle East crisis. One can only imagine the accolades he will receive for pulling off this agreement. He will receive the Nobel Peace Prize and be *Time*'s "Person of the Year." The perpetual, thorny Middle East crisis will appear to be solved.

With this guarantee of peace and protection, Israel will be able to relax and let its guard down for the first time in its modern history. Lulled into a false sense of security, Israel will direct its energies toward increased wealth rather than defense—only to have the peace treaty shattered in less than four years when the Russian-led assault force will strike the unsuspecting nation, fulfilling Ezekiel's prophecy.[20]

John Phillips summarizes the timing of this invasion in relation to other end-times events: "Only one period fits all the facts. When the Beast first comes to power in Europe, he will quickly unify the West, impose his totalitarian will on the nations under his control, and begin to prepare for world conquest. The major obstacle to his future plans will be a revitalized Russia." And, I might add, a radical Islamic presence. Phillips continues: "The invasion, then, takes place *after* the Rapture of the church, *after* the rise of the Beast in the West, *after* the signing of the pact with Israel, and just *before* the Beast takes over the world. Indeed it is the collapse of Russia [and its Islamic allies] that makes his global empire possible."[21]

David Jeremiah pinpoints the timing of this invasion: "To summarize, it will come after Israel returns to its homeland, after it has become highly prosperous, and after the implementation of the seven-year peace treaty with the Antichrist."[22]

THE RUSSIANS ARE COMING

Whatever view one holds of the timing of the coming Russian invasion, one thing is certain—it will happen. It may happen *soon* if the Rapture comes quickly and the Antichrist appears to bring peace to Israel, or even *sooner* if all the conditions in Ezekiel 38 are currently in place, as some believe.

The *timing* of Russia's offensive may be debated, but the *truth* of it is not up for discussion. God has spoken. And we see signs all around us that it could be very soon. The Jewish people are back in their land living in prosperity. Russia is taking its place on the world stage right on cue. World leaders continue to pursue a road map to Middle East peace. The signs are lighting up like runway lights signaling the coming of Jesus Christ.

As John Walvoord says, "The world today is like a stage being set for a great drama. The major actors are already in the wings waiting for their moment in history. The main stage props are already in place. The prophetic play could begin at any time. . . . Russia is poised to the north of the Holy Land for entry in the end-time conflict. . . . Each nation is ready to play out its role in the final hours of history."[23]

The time is at hand.

CHAPTER 9

WHAT DOES THE FUTURE HOLD?

THE BOARD IS SET, AND THE PIECES ARE MOVING.
GANDALF, THE RETURN OF THE KING

There's a famous story from Russian history about Grigory Alexandrovich Potemkin. He lived from 1739 to 1791 during the reign of Catherine the Great. He was a brilliant statesman and successful field marshal, conquering several new territories, creating new armies, and building up the Russian fleet. But he had one fatal flaw in his character—he exaggerated nearly everything he did. This trait reached its peak when he boasted incessantly to Catherine the Great about the construction projects he had undertaken in the outlying regions of Russia, especially in Crimea. He painted such a lavish picture of all the beautiful buildings that had been constructed that she decided she had to go see it all for herself.

Of course, this put Potemkin in quite a spot because it was all a lie. He left the city as quickly as possible, traveled to Crimea, and gathered thousands of people to build entire pasteboard villages—hollow facades of villages, like Hollywood props, along the desolate banks of the Dnieper River. Potemkin had people there walking up and down the streets at the time of the queen's visit. As the queen and her entourage passed by and were quickly paraded down the streets, they didn't notice that it was not a real city at all. It was all just a facade. Potemkin's standing was greatly enhanced in the eyes of Catherine the Great. To add even more intrigue to the story, most believe that even the story itself is a myth.

Nevertheless, there arose an expression—"Potemkin Village." A Potemkin Village is a facade, something that appears to have substance but has no reality. Since that time, the term Potemkin Village has come into our language to express that which is supposed to be something but is really nothing, something that appears elaborate and impressive but is a sham.

The prophecies of God's Word, including the prophecies about Russia in Ezekiel 38–39, are no Potemkin Village. They're not a myth. They're not imagination. They're not speculation. As David Jeremiah says, "We have good reason to believe the Russian threat is real. In fact, we have evidence that, at some point, Russia will ignite a pivotal world war like none ever seen or imagined. According to the prophet Ezekiel, this is a sure thing. Russia's aggressive moves today cast a long shadow into a future explicitly described in Ezekiel's prophecy."[1]

TIMES OF THE SIGNS

As we've seen, recent trends bear a remarkable correspondence to what Ezekiel predicted more than 2,500 years ago. Events are unfolding just as we should expect in light of Ezekiel's prophecy. As Charles Dyer and Mark Tobey say, "The parallels between Ezekiel's prophecy and events today are compelling, almost frighteningly so."[2]

The starting point for the prophetic panorama of events is Ezekiel 37, which predicts the regathering of the Jewish people to their land. Since 1948, the world has watched this prophecy come to fruition. Against all odds, after almost two thousand years of dispersion, the Jewish people are in the process of being regathered to their ancient homeland. About six million Jews reside in the Promised Land, sitting in the middle of a sea of enemies.

Ezekiel 37 forms the foundation for all that will follow. The regathering and restoration of the Jews to the Promised Land was a kind of "super sign" that set many gears in motion. Israel is God's timepiece—his clock. When we want to know where we are on God's prophetic timetable, the first place we need to look is Israel.

The presence of the Jewish people in their ancient land is the prerequisite for the unfolding of the end times. The event that commences the final seven years of Tribulation is the signing of a covenant between the final Antichrist and the Jewish people (see Daniel 9:27). For that to occur, there must be a nation of Israel. The rebirth of Israel in 1948 set the prophetic sequence in motion.

As Joel Rosenberg says, "Today, for the first time in two thousand years, we are seeing all of these signs come true, and the rebirth of Israel is the most dramatic sign of them all. We can, therefore, have confidence that Jesus' return is closer than ever. . . . It is true that Jesus cautions us not to speculate on the exact day and hour of his return. But we are encouraged to watch current events closely and know when the clock is running out."[3]

In addition to the rebirth of Israel, many other developments point toward the end-times scenario in Scripture. Globalism is paving the way for a one-world government and economy of the end times predicted in Revelation 13.

The Middle East is a hotbed of radicalism and turmoil. The attention of the world is focused there, just as we should anticipate if the end of days is getting close.

The Russian bear has roared out of hibernation suddenly and dramatically and dominates world headlines every day. The Bear's footprints continue to leave their mark all over the world.

Iran, the world's number-one sponsor of terrorism, is testing ballistic missiles at the same time it continues down the path toward nuclear capability. The Iran nuclear deal has temporarily stalled its nuclear development but only for a few years. Iran is Israel's most dangerous enemy. Its leaders make no effort to hide their malice toward Israel. Iran's Mahdi mentality fuels its expansionist ambitions as it works to hasten the coming of its messiah.

Turkey is descending into a dictatorship led by an Islamist and is cozying up to Russia and Iran. President Erdoğan's rhetoric against Israel is heating up. Four of the ancient allies named in Ezekiel 38 are located in modern Turkey.

The rise of ISIS and the civil war in Syria, while not the direct fulfillment of any biblical prophecies, are keeping the world focused on the Middle East. Syria is a flashpoint that is aligning Russia, Iran, and Turkey into a fearsome triumvirate. Russia and Iran have seized the chaos in Syria as an opportunity to bring in troops and air power, putting them just north of Israel.

Libya and Sudan are radical Islamic nations with deep animus toward Israel. The deepening turmoil and instability in these nations has provided an opening for greater Russian influence. These nations, too, are mentioned by Ezekiel.

The world desperately yearns for peace in the Middle East, primarily in Israel. The Bible says Israel will be at rest and secure when the Russian-led invasion occurs. The ongoing Middle East peace process could be a harbinger of the peace treaty the Antichrist will negotiate or at least confirm with Israel and her near enemies.

Never before have so many signs converged so quickly in such a short span of time that correspond to the matrix of end-times events predicted in Scripture. The pieces are moving.

The words of J. Vernon McGee are fitting: "I am seeing a stage being set for Russia's move against Israel. I do not know how close we are. I see not only one sign but the multiplication of all these signs about us and believe they are setting the stage. It looks as if God is getting ready to move again in the affairs of this earth."[4] Current events in Russia and the Middle East trace the trajectory that points toward the gathering storm of the Russian invasion of Israel—the War of Gog and Magog.

A PROPHETIC CHECKLIST

With all we've seen thus far, I thought it might be helpful to bring together all the key events and players in a simple chronology. The list below is a succinct summary of significant past and present world events that are part of the buildup to the end of days, a preview of what's next, and a forecast of where it's all headed.[5]

1. The modern state of Israel was established on May 14, 1948.
2. The Soviet Union, led by Russia, became a world superpower and an ally of the Islamic world.
3. The Middle East became the most significant trouble spot in the world and the hub of global terror.
4. The Iron Curtain fell in 1991, removing a major barrier to the revival of the Roman empire and the rise of the king of the west.

5. The 9/11 attacks on the United States began the war on terror, setting in motion a chain of events and bringing major realignment in the Middle East.

6. The world clamors for peace as continued turmoil, terror attacks, chaos, and instability plague the Middle East.

7. Russia has reemerged as a global force.

8. Ten leaders (the "Group of Ten") will emerge from a European and Mediterranean coalition, commencing the last phase of the final world empire.

9. In a bold power play, a new Mediterranean strongman (aka the Antichrist) will seize control of the powerful ten-leader group.

10. The Western leader will negotiate what appears to be a "final" peace settlement in the Middle East. The duration of the agreement will be seven years. Israel will feel secure and relax its defenses.

11. While all these events are transpiring, the king of the north—the Russian head of an alliance including Turkey and Iran—will emerge as a challenger to the Antichrist.

12. The king of the south—who will lead a North African coalition consisting of Egypt, Libya, Sudan, and possibly other nations—will come on the scene, allying his forces with the king of the north.

13. While Israel is at rest, Russia will ignite a surprise invasion to wipe out the Jewish people and challenge the king of the west. The Western nations

and moderate Arabs will raise a weak protest that's all words but no action. No one will come to Israel's defense, not even the United States.

14. When all looks lost for Israel, God will intervene, miraculously destroying the invaders. Russia's coalition will go up in smoke.

15. With the northern and southern alliances out of the way, the king of the west will take center stage, proclaim himself world dictator, break his peace agreement with Israel, and declare himself to be God.

16. The terrible judgments of the Great Tribulation will be poured out on the nations of the world as outlined in Revelation 6–18. The world will be plunged into a terrible time of wrath.

17. As the Antichrist's hold on power begins to slip, armies from throughout the world, including the kings of the east, will converge on the Middle East for the final world war. The armies will gather in northern Israel at Armageddon and spread all the way to Jerusalem.

18. Jesus Christ, the fifth and final King of the end times, will return to earth with his armies from heaven. He is the Word of God, the King of kings and Lord of lords, the Alpha and Omega, the Beginning and the End.

19. The armies of the world gathered at Armageddon will unite to resist Christ's coming and will be

obliterated in the Battle of Armageddon. Jesus will speak a word, and they will all wither under his presence.

20. Christ will establish his thousand-year reign on earth, and after his reign, God will create a new heaven and a new earth where God will dwell with his people forever.

What a forecast! What a future! That's where it's all headed. What's the world coming to? It's coming to the feet of Jesus. History is headed toward the feet of Jesus. Since everything is headed toward the feet of Jesus, we should humbly live our lives there now and keep looking for his coming.

THE BLESSED HOPE

In the days ahead, there will undoubtedly be many sudden, unexpected turns in world events. Headlines will come and go. Events will ebb and flow. Nations and leaders will rise and fall. Real news and fake news will continue to clarify and confuse. The drumbeat of wars and rumors of wars will quicken. But the Word of God will not change. What God has prophesied will come to pass, just as surely as hundreds of biblical prophecies have already been fulfilled. For this reason, as time runs out, our focus must always remain on the unchanging Word of the living God and the hope of Christ's coming. A. W. Tozer says it well:

Let us be alert to the season in which we are living. It is the season of the Blessed Hope. . . . It is imperative that we stay fully alert to the times in which we live. . . . All signs today point to this being the season of the Blessed Hope. . . . All around us, we have the evidence of Jesus' soon return. Each day our focus should be on the Coming One. Our focus on the Blessed Hope is the most important discipline of our Christian life.[6]

That's quite a statement. "The most important discipline of our Christian life" is to focus on the coming of Jesus Christ. That's humbling. How true is this in the lives of most followers of Christ? How true is this in your life . . . and in mine? With all we see happening today, we have more reason than any previous generation to observe this discipline and to keep our focus on the Blessed Hope. No previous generation has seen anything compared to what we're witnessing every day.

Professor and prophecy expert Ed Hindson reminds us of the urgency of our times: "God's clock, the clock of history, is ticking away. It never speeds up and never slows down. It just keeps on ticking, continually and relentlessly, moving us closer and closer to the end of the age. How close we are to the end will only be revealed by time itself. Don't gamble with your eternal destiny. Time may very well be running out."[7]

Time *is* running out. The return of Christ could be very soon. But how soon?

CHAPTER 10

IT'S ALWAYS SOON

---

*HE WHO IS THE FAITHFUL WITNESS TO ALL THESE THINGS [JESUS] SAYS,
"YES, I AM COMING SOON!"*
REVELATION 22:20

In C. S. Lewis's *The Voyage of the Dawn Treader,* Aslan, the lion who is the Christ figure in the story, tells Lucy that he will have to go away. He reassures her by saying, "Do not look so sad. We shall meet soon again."

Lucy, concerned about when she will next see him, asks, "Please, Aslan, what do you call *soon?*"

And Aslan replies, "I call all times soon."[1]

Jesus is coming soon. He can come back at any time—any moment. Let those words sink in. Do we really believe he's coming? Do we believe he could come today? Do we live like we believe that? Is the truth of meeting him at any moment transforming your life and my life?

As I write and speak about end-times prophecy, I try to remind myself often of the wise words of Warren Wiersbe: "The purpose of Bible prophecy is not for us to make a calendar, but to build character."[2]

We've looked at Scripture's forecast for Russia's part in the end times. We've seen how God has set the stage for Russia to rise right on cue. This book is evidence that I believe in discerning legitimate signs of the times, but I believe even more strongly that we must never get so consumed with the signs that we forget the Savior. Christ must be our consuming passion. Meeting him must be our motivation. We're waiting for a person. We must never allow ourselves to get so focused on what will happen and when it will happen that we forget how it must change us to be more like him. We must never get so enamored with *timing* that we neglect *transformation*.

Studying the truth of Bible prophecy was never intended just to stir our emotions, satisfy our curiosity, or fill our heads with knowledge. The prophetic Scripture is given to fill us with hope and move us to a sense of urgency and action as we watch and wait for Jesus to come. Over the years, I've been surprised to hear many people demean the study of Bible prophecy, calling it impractical, unrelated to everyday life, or simply a scare tactic. This attitude is unfounded. A. W. Tozer reminds us, "The point of Bible prophecy is not to alarm us but to alert us to the circumstances leading up to the Lord's return. This alertness is to spur us on to be ready; and the Bible says a lot about how we can be ready for His return."[3]

Every time the New Testament gives any substantial

teaching about the end times, it is always accompanied by practical application of that truth to our daily lives. Few things are more practical than prophecy. Paul Benware shares this sentiment:

> Does this doctrinal area of Bible prophecy make a difference? Yes, emphatically yes! God wants us to know many truths about what is going to take place in the future, and He wants those truths to change us right now in the present. He desires that prophetic truth change the way we think, the way we behave, and the way we view Him.[4]

God wants us to know the prophetic Scripture. The sheer volume of prophecy makes that clear. Almost 30 percent of the Bible was prophecy at the time it was written. If God didn't want us to study prophecy and know the future, he would have omitted that 30 percent. However, our knowledge of prophecy, like all biblical knowledge, must transform us. We must be faithful doers of the Word (see James 1:22-25).

There are many positive effects that result from anticipating Christ's coming, but I want to leave you with five simple points to apply to your life.

LET THE EXPECTATION OF CHRIST'S COMING CONVERT YOU

If you have never accepted Jesus Christ as your Savior, that's the first life-changing step you need to take. Everything begins here. You need the forgiveness of sins and new life that Jesus offers more than you've ever needed anything else. God's gracious answer to mankind's desperate plight is found in the death and resurrection of Jesus Christ. At the cross, Jesus, who is without sin, bore the sin of all humanity. He took your sins. He took my sins. The Bible says, "God made Christ, who never sinned, to be the offering for our sin, so that we could be made right with God through Christ" (2 Corinthians 5:21).

In taking our place on the cross, Jesus exhausted God's just wrath against human sin, leaving God free to extend his grace and mercy to all who will come in simple, childlike faith to trust and receive Jesus. Speaking of Jesus, Scripture says, "To all who believed him and accepted him, he gave the right to become children of God" (John 1:12). We become God's children by receiving his Son, Jesus.

In *Fresh Illustrations for Preaching and Teaching*, there's a great story about the mighty Niagara Falls, where the Niagara River plummets some 180 feet at the American and Horseshoe Falls. "Before the falls, there are violent, turbulent rapids. Farther upstream, however, where the river's current flows more gently, boats are able to navigate. Just before the Welland River empties into the Niagara, a pedestrian walkway spans the river. Posted on this bridge's pylons is a warning sign for all boaters: 'Do you have an anchor?' followed by, 'Do you know how to use it?'" The author concludes, "Faith, like an anchor, is something we need to have and use to avoid spiritual cataclysm."[5]

That's true for every person—including you and me.

Without Christ, we're all in a boat helplessly headed for the falls. Our only hope is an anchor. Jesus is our anchor, and faith is how we access that anchor. The questions for every reader are simple: Do you have an anchor? Do you know how to use it?

Make sure you have faith in Jesus Christ as your Savior from sin. Let the truths of what lies ahead move you to accept Christ. If you have never accepted the grace of the Lord Jesus, you can do so right now by calling upon the Lord to save you. There are no magic words that bring salvation. It's the attitude of the heart and mind that really matters. But a simple prayer like this one can serve as an expression of faith in Christ. Why not pray these words if you've never done so before?

> Father, I know I'm a sinner. I know I cannot save myself. I need a Savior, and I believe Jesus is the Savior I need. I believe he died for me and rose from the dead. I trust in him alone to wash away my sins and give me eternal life. Amen.

If you prayed that prayer and it expresses the desire of your heart, the Bible says you've become a child of God. You have an anchor that will never fail you. Find a loving church that teaches the Bible, get baptized, read your Bible every day, and begin to serve the Lord in whatever way you can.

For those who already know the Lord, there are other effects the study of Bible prophecy and Christ's coming should have on our daily lives.

LET THE EXPECTATION OF CHRIST'S COMING COMFORT YOU

An Arab proverb says, "Death is a black camel that kneels at every door." Sorrow is no respecter of persons. It comes to every person on earth at one time or another. Our only hope when the grim reaper strikes is the hope of Christ's resurrection and second coming. Jesus is our supreme comfort and encouragement when death hits close to home. The apostle Paul reminds us that while we may weep at the grave, we don't have to fear the grave. Death doesn't have the last word:

> Now, dear brothers and sisters, we want you to know what will happen to the believers who have died so you will not grieve like people who have no hope. For since we believe that Jesus died and was raised to life again, we also believe that when Jesus returns, God will bring back with him the believers who have died.
>
> We tell you this directly from the Lord: We who are still living when the Lord returns will not meet him ahead of those who have died. For the Lord himself will come down from heaven with a commanding shout, with the voice of the archangel, and with the trumpet call of God. First, the believers who have died will rise from their graves. Then, together with them, we who are still alive and remain on the earth will be caught up in the clouds to meet the Lord in the air. Then we will be with the Lord forever. So encourage each other with these words.
>
> 1 THESSALONIANS 4:13-18

The Lord's coming comforts and consoles us with the assurance of ultimate resurrection and reunion with our loved ones. When a believer dies, we don't say "good-bye," just "good night."

I had the privilege of knowing Tim LaHaye, coauthor of the bestselling Left Behind series. Several times I've heard him tell the story of his father's death, when Tim was only nine years old. As you can imagine, the sudden loss of his father had a lasting impact on his life. Tim was in despair, but the pastor officiating the funeral delivered a message that gave young Tim hope: "This is not the end of Frank LaHaye; because he accepted Jesus Christ, the day will come when the Lord will shout from heaven and descend, and the dead in Christ will rise first and then we'll be caught up together to meet him in the air." Tim often recounted how, once he heard these words, "all of a sudden, there was hope in my heart I'd see my father again."

That's the comforting hope Christ brings.

LET THE EXPECTATION OF CHRIST'S COMING CALM YOU

On many fronts, our world today seems to be spinning out of control. Fear and anxiety about the future is mounting. People are searching for ways to cope. The night before he died on the cross, Jesus spoke these words to his closest followers, but they apply to our lives today just as much:

Don't let your hearts be troubled. Trust in God, and trust also in me. There is more than enough room in

my Father's home. If this were not so, would I have
told you that I am going to prepare a place for you?
When everything is ready, I will come and get you,
so that you will always be with me where I am.

JOHN 14:1-3

What a challenge in our world today. "Don't let your
hearts be troubled." Jesus is telling us that we can remain
calm and stable in the midst of troubled times, knowing
where everything is headed and knowing that he can come
at any moment to take us home.

LET THE EXPECTATION OF CHRIST'S COMING CONTROL YOU

After an extended section describing the any-moment rapture of believers to meet Jesus, the apostle Paul concludes
with this challenge: "So, my dear brothers and sisters, be
strong and immovable. Always work enthusiastically for the
Lord, for you know that nothing you do for the Lord is ever
useless" (1 Corinthians 15:58). Knowing that Jesus can come
at any time serves as a powerful, pressing motivation and
incentive to sacrificially serve him. We know that what we
do for him won't be in vain because his coming for us is sure.

Allow the hope of Christ's coming to control your life.
Get involved in a local church that preaches the gospel and
teaches the Bible. Find a place to serve there. The Bible
tells us that every believer has at least one spiritual gift, that
is, a divine enablement to carry out some function with

ease and effectiveness to serve others (see Romans 12:6-8; 1 Corinthians 12:8-10, 28-29; Ephesians 4:11-12). Read these passages in your Bible, and ask the Lord to guide you into a place of effective, empowered service. Listen to others who will affirm and confirm what you're gifted to do.

Jesus is coming. Your sacrifice and service won't be in vain. "Work enthusiastically for the Lord." It will be worth it.

LET THE EXPECTATION OF CHRIST'S COMING CLEANSE YOU

To borrow a phrase from Judge Robert Bork, our culture today is "slouching towards Gomorrah." We see it on every front. Morality is sliding, and decadence—even outright depravity—seems more and more to be accepted and even applauded. Everywhere we turn, it seems our culture is coarsening and corroding. Sadly, even in the lives of many professing Christians, there seems to be a major disconnect between what is professed and what is practiced. Moral malaise surrounds us.

None of us are perfect in our efforts no matter how hard we try. We all fail far more than we would like. Our lack of faithfulness is humbling. Yet in spite of our frailty, our goal is to please the Lord in what we do, what we say, and what we think. The hope of Christ's coming is a powerful yet often neglected incentive to live as a pure vessel. You might be surprised what a close connection exists between prophecy and practical living in the New Testament. Here are four texts that underscore the purifying power of prophecy. Please read them thoughtfully.

We are instructed to turn from godless living and sinful pleasures. We should live in this evil world with wisdom, righteousness, and devotion to God, while we look forward with hope to that wonderful day when the glory of our great God and Savior, Jesus Christ, will be revealed. He gave his life to free us from every kind of sin, to cleanse us, and to make us his very own people, totally committed to doing good deeds.

TITUS 2:12-14

Dear friends, we are already God's children, but he has not yet shown us what we will be like when Christ appears. But we do know that we will be like him, for we will see him as he really is. And all who have this eager expectation will keep themselves pure, just as he is pure.

I JOHN 3:2-3

Since everything around us is going to be destroyed like this, what holy and godly lives you should live, looking forward to the day of God and hurrying it along. On that day, he will set the heavens on fire, and the elements will melt away in the flames. But we are looking forward to the new heavens and new earth he has promised, a world filled with God's righteousness.

And so, dear friends, while you are waiting for these things to happen, make every effort to

be found living peaceful lives that are pure and
blameless in his sight.

2 PETER 3:11-14

This is all the more urgent, for you know how late it
is; time is running out. Wake up, for our salvation is
nearer now than when we first believed. The night is
almost gone; the day of salvation will soon be here.
So remove your dark deeds like dirty clothes, and
put on the shining armor of right living. Because
we belong to the day, we must live decent lives for
all to see. Don't participate in the darkness of wild
parties and drunkenness, or in sexual promiscuity
and immoral living, or in quarreling and jealousy.
Instead, clothe yourself with the presence of the Lord
Jesus Christ. And don't let yourself think about ways
to indulge your evil desires.

ROMANS 13:11-14

The close connection in these passages between anticipating
the coming of the Lord and holy living is striking. What this
means is that any believer who gets up in the morning thinking
Jesus could come today will strive to please the Lord. It's a fail-
safe formula. Yet the opposite is also true. Failure to live expec-
tantly makes us far more vulnerable to temptation and sin.

Charles Haddon Spurgeon, the eminent English pastor,
cites the any-moment expectancy of Christ's coming as an
energizing force:

I feel rebuked, myself, sometimes, for not watching
for my Master when I know that, at this very time,
my dogs are sitting against the door, waiting for me—
and long before I reach home, there they will be and,
at the first sound of the carriage wheels, they will lift
up their voices with delight because their master is
coming home! Oh, if we loved our Lord as dogs love
their masters, how we should catch the first sound of
His Coming—and be waiting, always waiting—and
never happy until at last we should see Him! Pardon
me for using a dog as a picture of what you ought to
be, but when you have attained to a state above that, I
will find another illustration to explain my meaning.[6]

Spurgeon puts us in our place, but he also gives this
impassioned plea:

Oh, Beloved, let us try, every morning, to get up
as if that were the morning in which Christ would
come! And when we go up to bed at night, may
we lie down with this thought, "Perhaps I shall be
awakened by the ringing out of the silver trumpets
heralding His Coming. Before the sun arises, I may
be startled from my dreams by the greatest of all
cries, 'The Lord is come! The Lord is come!'" What a
check, what an incentive, what a bridle, what a spur
such thoughts as these would be to us! Take this for
the guide of your whole life—act as if Jesus would

come during the act in which you are engaged—and if you would not wish to be caught in that act by the Coming of the Lord, let it not be your act.[7]

Jesus is coming. Only the time is uncertain. As J. Dwight Pentecost encourages us, "May the joy of looking for Him produce in us a holy life so that we will not be ashamed when we see Him."[8]

LIVE LOOKING

In his excellent book *Is This the End?* David Jeremiah issues this challenge from the past to the current generation:

I have heard it said that when first-century Christians traveled from city to city, they would stop at every crossroads and look in all directions, always anticipating the possibility that they might see Christ returning. The ensuing centuries seem to have dulled that imminent expectation, but they should not. We must ever be aware that the Rapture could occur at any moment.[9]

The current rumblings in Russia and the Middle East can spark terror, but they can also spark a hunger for Christ's return. We know that God is in control, and we know that Jesus is coming back for his church. He tells us, "Yes, I am coming soon!" (Revelation 22:20).

Remember: with Jesus, it's always soon!

May he find us focused and faithful when he comes.

EZEKIEL 38–39

The following text is chapters 38 and 39 of the biblical book Ezekiel. What follows is the New Living Translation, the translation I've used in most of the book. In a few places where my interpretation differs from the New Living Translation, I've left notes to this effect. I hope this passage of Scripture will help you to understand what I've written in this book about Russia's rise in the end times.

CHAPTER 38

A Message for Gog

¹This is another message that came to me from the LORD: ²"Son of man, turn and face Gog of the land of Magog, the prince who rules over† the nations of Meshech and Tubal, and prophesy against him. ³Give him this message from the Sovereign LORD: Gog, I am your enemy! ⁴I will turn you

---

† See chapter 3, where I discuss the term *rosh*. The NLT translates the Hebrew word *rosh* as "who rules over." NASB has "of Rosh," which, as I discuss in chapter 3, is the name of a place currently occupied by Russia. The word *rosh* also occurs in 38:3 and 39:1.

around and put hooks in your jaws to lead you out with your whole army—your horses and charioteers in full armor and a great horde armed with shields and swords. ⁵Persia, Ethiopia, and Libya will join you, too, with all their weapons. ⁶Gomer and all its armies will also join you, along with the armies of Beth-togarmah from the distant north, and many others.

⁷"Get ready; be prepared! Keep all the armies around you mobilized, and take command of them. ⁸A long time from now you will be called into action. In the distant future you will swoop down on the land of Israel, which will be enjoying peace after recovering from war and after its people have returned from many lands to the mountains of Israel. ⁹You and all your allies—a vast and awesome army—will roll down on them like a storm and cover the land like a cloud.

¹⁰"This is what the Sovereign Lord says: At that time evil thoughts will come to your mind, and you will devise a wicked scheme. ¹¹You will say, 'Israel is an unprotected land filled with unwalled villages! I will march against her and destroy these people who live in such confidence! ¹²I will go to those formerly desolate cities that are now filled with people who have returned from exile in many nations. I will capture vast amounts of plunder, for the people are rich with livestock and other possessions now. They think the whole world revolves around them!' ¹³But Sheba and Dedan and the merchants of Tarshish will ask, 'Do you really think the armies you have gathered can rob them of silver and gold? Do you think you can drive away their livestock and seize their goods and carry off plunder?'

[14]"Therefore, son of man, prophesy against Gog. Give him this message from the Sovereign LORD: When my people are living in peace in their land, then you will rouse yourself. [15]You will come from your homeland in the distant north with your vast cavalry and your mighty army, [16]and you will attack my people Israel, covering their land like a cloud. At that time in the distant future, I will bring you against my land as everyone watches, and my holiness will be displayed by what happens to you, Gog. Then all the nations will know that I am the LORD.

[17]"This is what the Sovereign LORD asks: Are you the one I was talking about long ago, when I announced through Israel's prophets that in the future I would bring you against my people? [18]But this is what the Sovereign LORD says: When Gog invades the land of Israel, my fury will boil over! [19]In my jealousy and blazing anger, I promise a mighty shaking in the land of Israel on that day. [20]All living things—the fish in the sea, the birds of the sky, the animals of the field, the small animals that scurry along the ground, and all the people on earth—will quake in terror at my presence. Mountains will be thrown down; cliffs will crumble; walls will fall to the earth. [21]I will summon the sword against you on all the hills of Israel, says the Sovereign LORD. Your men will turn their swords against each other. [22]I will punish you and your armies with disease and bloodshed; I will send torrential rain, hailstones, fire, and burning sulfur! [23]In this way, I will show my greatness and holiness, and I will make myself known to all the nations of the world. Then they will know that I am the LORD.

CHAPTER 39

The Slaughter of Gog's Hordes

¹"Son of man, prophesy against Gog. Give him this message from the Sovereign Lord: I am your enemy, O Gog, ruler of the nations of Meshech and Tubal. ²I will turn you around and drive you toward the mountains of Israel, bringing you from the distant north. ³I will knock the bow from your left hand and the arrows from your right hand, and I will leave you helpless. ⁴You and your army and your allies will all die on the mountains. I will feed you to the vultures and wild animals. ⁵You will fall in the open fields, for I have spoken, says the Sovereign Lord. ⁶And I will rain down fire on Magog and on all your allies who live safely on the coasts. Then they will know that I am the Lord.

⁷"In this way, I will make known my holy name among my people of Israel. I will not let anyone bring shame on it. And the nations, too, will know that I am the Lord, the Holy One of Israel. ⁸That day of judgment will come, says the Sovereign Lord. Everything will happen just as I have declared it.

⁹"Then the people in the towns of Israel will go out and pick up your small and large shields, bows and arrows, javelins and spears, and they will use them for fuel. There will be enough to last them seven years! ¹⁰They won't need to cut wood from the fields or forests, for these weapons will give them all the fuel they need. They will plunder those who planned to plunder them, and they will rob those who planned to rob them, says the Sovereign Lord.

[11] "And I will make a vast graveyard for Gog and his hordes in the Valley of the Travelers, east of the Dead Sea. It will block the way of those who travel there, and they will change the name of the place to the Valley of Gog's Hordes. [12] It will take seven months for the people of Israel to bury the bodies and cleanse the land. [13] Everyone in Israel will help, for it will be a glorious victory for Israel when I demonstrate my glory on that day, says the Sovereign LORD.

[14] "After seven months, teams of men will be appointed to search the land for skeletons to bury, so the land will be made clean again. [15] Whenever bones are found, a marker will be set up so the burial crews will take them to be buried in the Valley of Gog's Hordes. [16] (There will be a town there named Hamonah, which means 'horde.') And so the land will finally be cleansed.

[17] "And now, son of man, this is what the Sovereign LORD says: Call all the birds and wild animals. Say to them: Gather together for my great sacrificial feast. Come from far and near to the mountains of Israel, and there eat flesh and drink blood! [18] Eat the flesh of mighty men and drink the blood of princes as though they were rams, lambs, goats, and bulls—all fattened animals from Bashan! [19] Gorge yourselves with flesh until you are glutted; drink blood until you are drunk. This is the sacrificial feast I have prepared for you. [20] Feast at my banquet table—feast on horses and charioteers, on mighty men and all kinds of valiant warriors, says the Sovereign LORD.

[21] "In this way, I will demonstrate my glory to the nations.

Everyone will see the punishment I have inflicted on them and the power of my fist when I strike. [22]And from that time on the people of Israel will know that I am the LORD their God. [23]The nations will then know why Israel was sent away to exile—it was punishment for sin, for they were unfaithful to their God. Therefore, I turned away from them and let their enemies destroy them. [24]I turned my face away and punished them because of their defilement and their sins.

Restoration for God's People

[25]"So now, this is what the Sovereign LORD says: I will end the captivity of my people; I will have mercy on all Israel, for I jealously guard my holy reputation! [26]They will accept responsibility for their past shame and unfaithfulness after they come home to live in peace in their own land, with no one to bother them. [27]When I bring them home from the lands of their enemies, I will display my holiness among them for all the nations to see. [28]Then my people will know that I am the LORD their God, because I sent them away to exile and brought them home again. I will leave none of my people behind. [29]And I will never again turn my face from them, for I will pour out my Spirit upon the people of Israel. I, the Sovereign LORD, have spoken!"

THE KING OF THE NORTH: THE NORTHERN CONFEDERACY

BY DR. JOHN F. WALVOORD

In my books I like to expose the readers to some of the scholars and giants of Bible prophecy who have influenced my thinking and shaped my own views. Dr. John Walvoord was one of those men. His book The Nations in Prophecy *was first published in 1967. I read it for the first time in 1985, and it had a formative impact on my understanding of Ezekiel 38–39.*

I've quoted this book a few times in Russia Rising, *but I thought it would be helpful to include Dr. Walvoord's chapter on Ezekiel 38–39 for you to read. Some of the material goes over ground I've covered but does so in a different way. Also, I often find that reading something stated in different words can reinforce its meaning.*

I hope you enjoy reading this chapter as much as I have over the years.

In the warfare that characterizes the end of the age, the Scriptures predict a great world conflict which eventually involves all the nations of the earth. In the Scriptures that portray these stirring events, three major crises may be observed. First, a crisis in the Mediterranean area leads to the formation of the revived Roman Empire composed of a ten-nation confederacy. This is occasioned by the rise of the Roman "prince that shall come" (Daniel 9:26) who subdues three of the kings and secures the submission of the seven remaining rulers. His successful conquest of these ten kingdoms, outlined in Daniel 7:23-26, makes the Roman ruler supreme in his control of this revived form of the ancient Roman Empire.

The second phase of the struggle is recorded in Ezekiel 38 and 39. The great battle there described may be the forerunner of the expansion of the Roman Empire from domination of the Mediterranean area to the role of a world empire embracing all nations of the earth (cp. Daniel 7:23; Revelation 13:7, 8). The third phase of the world struggle is at the end of the great tribulation period just before the second coming of Christ, when major sections of the world rebel against the Roman ruler as their leader. A gigantic world war ensues with the Holy Land as its focal point (Daniel 11:40-45; Revelation 16:12-16).

Expositors are by no means agreed as to the precise details of these events or their place in the sequence. It is possible, however, to be sure about such facts as the geographic origination of military forces which converge upon the Holy Land, described as coming from the north, the east, and the south. All of these forces seem to be in opposition to the Roman ruler who may be called the king of the west, although the Scriptures never assign him this title.

The prophet Daniel in his summary of the world struggle which ends the age declares: "And at the time of the end shall the king of the south push at him: and the king of the north shall come against him like a whirlwind, with chariots, and with horsemen, and with many ships; and he shall enter into the countries, and shall overflow and pass over" (Daniel 11:40). The reference to the king of the north in this passage raises the question concerning Russia and other countries to the north of the Holy Land which figure in this final world struggle. A major contribution to this subject is found in the prophecies of Ezekiel concerning a great invasion of the Holy Land from the north in the end time.

THE RISE OF RUSSIA IN THE TWENTIETH CENTURY

One of the significant aspects of modern life which all have observed in the last quarter of a century is the remarkable rise of Russia to a place of world prominence. At the close of World War II, Russia as a nation was crushed, its manpower destroyed, its cities in ruin. It was a nation that would have been utterly defeated if it had not been for American help. Since World War II, Russia has recovered and has become a prominent nation with world-wide influence which few nations have ever achieved. Today, Russia is one of the principal competitors of the United States of America for world fame and world leadership. Through the instrument of communism and nations which share Russia's convictions on communism, almost half of the world's population is in some sense or other in the Russian orbit. Such a phenomenal rise of a nation so godless and blasphemous must have some prophetic significance.

DOES THE BIBLE CONTAIN PROPHECY ABOUT RUSSIA?

In the study of prophecy, care must be taken not to create doctrine without proper Scriptural support. Many aspects of prophecy in the Bible may be understood only partially. There are great themes of prophecy, however, which do not rest on isolated texts, but upon extended portions of the Word of God. As these Scriptures are studied, some settled conclusions can be reached regarding the main movements of God in the prophetic future.

The word *Russia* is not found in the English Bible, and at first glance it would seem that there is nothing in the Bible that would give any information about Russia. A more careful investigation, however, reveals that there are two long chapters in the Bible which seem to concern themselves with the nation Russia, with certain other portions of Scripture which cast added light upon the subject. Not only has the Bible something to say about Russia, but what it reveals is of tremendous significance in God's prophetic program.

In Ezekiel 38 and 39, a description is given of a war between Israel and a nation which many have identified as Russia. The two chapters mentioned describe the invasion of the land of Israel by the armies of Russia and the nations that are associated with her. The Scriptures are plain that this is a military invasion and reveal many details about the situation existing at the time of that invasion. The dramatic outcome of the battle is the utter destruction of the army that invades the land of Israel. Written by the prophet Ezekiel, who himself was in exile from the land of Israel, this prophecy was inspired by the Spirit of God. A natural question can be raised, however, inasmuch as this was written some twenty-five hundred years ago, whether this passage has already been fulfilled.

The land of Israel has been the scene of many wars, and invasions have come from various parts of the world, north, east, and south. Many times the march of soldiers' feet has been heard crossing the little nation of Israel. The Bible records some of these wars and some of them have occurred since the canon of Scripture was closed. It would be difficult to examine the details of all these wars; however, if one did, he would find that none of them correspond to this prophecy. There never has been a war with Israel which fulfills the prophecies of Ezekiel 38 and 39. If one believes that the Bible is the Word of God and that it is infallible and must be fulfilled, the only logical conclusion is that this portion of Scripture, like many others, is still due a future fulfillment.

THE IDENTIFICATION OF RUSSIA

In beginning the study of this chapter, it is necessary to establish beyond any question that this passage deals with the nation Russia, inasmuch as the term itself does not occur.

There are a number of important factors which lead to the conclusion that the only nation which could possibly fulfill the specifications of these two chapters is the nation Russia. In the study of this chapter the American Standard Version will be used because of its clarification of certain difficult passages.

First of all, it is important to note the geographic description which is given. The terms "king of the north" and "king of the south" were used in Daniel 11:5-35 to describe the rulers to the north and south of Palestine who engaged in constant warfare in the second and third centuries B.C. This is now fulfilled prophecy. The king of the north and king of the south of Daniel 11:40-45, however, are future rulers involved in warfare in the end time. This is still unfulfilled prophecy. Ezekiel 38 and 39 fit into this future picture.

According to Ezekiel, the invading armies come to the land of Israel from "the uttermost part of the north" or as we would put it from the far north. In the Authorized Version the expression is translated merely "from the north," but in the more literal translation of the Hebrew found in the American Standard Version it is rendered, "the uttermost parts of the north," i.e., the extreme north. The important point is that it designates not merely the direction from which the army attacks Israel, but specifies the geographic origination of the army from a territory located in the far north. The house of Togarmah, one of the nations that is associated with Russia in this invasion, also comes from "the uttermost parts of the north" (Ezekiel 38:6).

A similar statement concerning the invader is made in verse 15, "Thou shalt come from thy place out of the uttermost parts of the north, thou, and many peoples with thee, all of them riding upon horses, a great company and a mighty army" (ASV). Again in Ezekiel 39:2, God says to them, "I will turn thee about, and will lead thee on, and will cause thee to come up from the uttermost parts of the north; and I will bring thee upon the mountains of Israel" (ASV). Three times in these chapters this army is stated to come from the extreme north.

If one takes any map of the world and draws a line north of the land of Israel he will inevitably come to the nation Russia. As soon as the line is drawn to the far north beyond Asia Minor and the Black Sea it is in Russia and continues to be in Russia for many hundreds of miles all the way to the Arctic Circle. Russia today spreads east and west some 6,000 miles, and one cannot escape Russia if he goes north of the Holy Land. On the basis of geography alone, it seems quite clear that the only nation which could possibly be referred to as coming from the far north would be the nation Russia. The suggestion that the nation is ancient Assyria revived is rendered improbable by the geographic description.

As the Scriptures are further examined, not only geographic data but also some confirming linguistic evidence is discovered. In the opening portion of Ezekiel 38, in verses 1 through 6, some names are mentioned which identify the invaders. This portion indicates that the Word of the Lord came to Ezekiel saying,

Son of man, set thy face toward Gog, of the land of
Magog, the prince of Rosh, Meshech, and Tubal, and
prophesy against him, and say, Thus saith the Lord
Jehovah: Behold, I am against thee, O Gog, prince
of Rosh, Meshech, and Tubal: and I will turn thee
about, and put hooks into thy jaws, and I will bring
thee forth, and all thine army, horses and horsemen,
all of them clothed in full armor, a great company
with buckler and shield, all of them handling
swords: Persia, Cush and Put with them, all of them
with shield and helmet; Gomer, and all his hordes;
the house of Togarmah in the uttermost parts of the
north, and all his hordes; even many peoples with
thee (ASV).

Most of the terms in this portion of Scripture are quite
strange to us and do not immediately connote anything relat-
ing to Russia. Certain facts are discovered as the passage is
examined more particularly. This portion of Scripture is a
message from God delivered by the prophet Ezekiel, directed
to a person whose name is Gog, who is described as of the
land of Magog and apparently the ruler of this land. The
term "Magog" is mentioned in Genesis 10:2. There we learn
that Magog was the second son of Japheth, the son of Noah.

Magog is best identified with the Scythians, a people
descended from Magog. The ancient historian Josephus
makes that identification and we have no reason to question
it. The Scythians apparently lived immediately to the north

of what was later to be the land of Israel, then some of them emigrated north, going all the way to the Arctic Circle. In other words, their posterity was scattered precisely over the geographical area that today is called Russia.

In Ezekiel 38 Gog is described as "the prince of Rosh" (ASV). The Authorized Version expresses it as the "chief prince." The translation, "the prince of Rosh," is a more literal rendering of the Hebrew. "Rosh" may be the root of the modern term, Russia. In the study of how ancient words come into modern language, it is quite common for the consonants to remain the same and the vowels to be changed. In the word "Rosh," if the vowel "o" is changed to "u" it becomes the root of the modern word, Russia, with the suffix added. In other words, the word itself seems to be an early form of the word from which the modern word, Russia, comes. Gesenius, the famous lexicographer, gives the assurance that this is a proper identification, that is, that Rosh is an early form of the word from which we get Russia.

The two terms, "Meshech" and "Tubal," also correspond to some prominent words in Russia. The term "Meshech" is similar to the modern name Moscow, and "Tubal," obviously, is similar to the name of one of the prominent Asiatic provinces of Russia, the province of Tobolsk. When this evidence is put together, it points to the conclusion that these terms are early references to portions of Russia, and therefore, the geographic argument is reinforced by the linguistic argument and supports the idea that this invading force comes from Russia.

As the prophecy is examined further it becomes obvious that the invaders utterly disregard God, because any nation that attacks the nation of Israel by so much is disregarding the Word of God. The godlessness of the invading army attacking Israel also points the finger to the nation Russia. On the basis of these three arguments, the geographic argument, the linguistic argument, and what might be called the theological argument, it may be concluded that the reference is to the nation Russia. In fact, there is no other reasonable alternative. Russia is today the only nation which seems to fit the picture.

A number of nations are associated with Russia in the invasion, but not too much is known about them. Persia, of course, is in that general area. Cush is another name for Ethiopia, which poses a problem because today Ethiopia is to the south. The term *Cush* may have been applied to other geographic areas, including that to the north of the land of Israel. The term, "Put," is a difficult expression about which little is known. In verse 6 the term, "Gomer," is identified by most as referring to the ancient Cimmerians, a portion of whom lived in what today is called southern or western Germany. Togarmah is commonly recognized as referring to the Armenians, who at one time lived immediately north of the land of Israel, and they, too, to some extent emigrated to the north. The nations which accompany Russia, for the most part, fit properly into the picture of assisting Russia in this invasion of the land of Israel.

THE PREDICTED INVASION OF ISRAEL

The actual invasion is described in Ezekiel 38:8-12. Some of the distinctive facts mentioned about the particular situation which will exist when this war begins are of utmost significance in the light of the world situation today. In this passage the "thou" refers throughout to Russia or to Gog. The term "they" is used to refer to Israel. Beginning in verse 8 and continuing through verse 16, the passage reads as follows:

> After many days thou shalt be visited: in the latter years thou shalt come into the land that is brought back from the sword, that is gathered out of many peoples, upon the mountains of Israel, which have been a continual waste; but it is brought forth out of the peoples, and they shall dwell securely, all of them. And thou shalt ascend, thou shalt come like a storm, thou shalt be like a cloud to cover the land, thou, and all thy hordes, and many peoples with thee.
>
> Thus saith the Lord Jehovah: It shall come to pass in that day, that things shall come into thy mind, and thou shalt devise an evil device: and thou shalt say, I will go up to the land of unwalled villages; I will go to them that are at rest, that dwell securely, all of them dwelling without walls, and having neither bars nor gates; to take the spoil and to take the prey; to turn thy hand against the waste places that are now inhabited, and against the people that

are gathered out of the nations, that have gotten cattle and goods, that dwell in the middle of the earth. Sheba, and Dedan, and the merchants of Tarshish, with all the young lions thereof, shall say unto thee, Art thou come to take the spoil? hast thou assembled thy company to take the prey? to carry away silver and gold, to take away cattle and goods, to take great spoil?

Therefore, son of man, prophesy, and say unto Gog, Thus saith the Lord Jehovah: In that day when my people Israel dwelleth securely, shalt thou not know it? And thou shalt come from thy place out of the uttermost parts of the north, thou, and many peoples with thee, all of them riding upon horses, a great company and a mighty army; and thou shalt come up against my people Israel, as a cloud to cover the land: it shall come to pass in the latter days, that I will bring thee against my land, that the nations may know me, when I shall be sanctified in thee, O Gog, before their eyes (ASV).

INVASION AFTER ISRAEL'S REGATHERING

Some highly significant facts are given in the above passage concerning the precise situation existing when the invasion takes place. There are a number of references to the fact that the people of Israel are back in their ancient land. This of course is of tremendous importance because it is only in our generation that the people of Israel have gone back to their ancient land. In A.D. 70, Titus, the Roman general, conquered Jerusalem, utterly destroyed it, and killed up to a million of the Jews. Roman soldiers later systematically went throughout the entire land of Israel destroying every building, sawing down or uprooting every tree, and doing everything they could to make the land totally uninhabitable. The result was that the land of Israel lay in waste for several generations. The children of Israel from that day to this have been scattered over the face of the earth.

At the close of World War II the children of Israel began to return to their ancient land in large numbers. Some had gone earlier, but they were few in number. They built up their strength and numbers until finally they were recognized as a nation in May, 1948. At that time one million Jews were back in their ancient land, the largest return since the days of the Exodus. In the years since, their number has doubled, and today there are two million Israelites under their own flag, speaking the Hebrew language, and reviving and restoring their ancient land to a scene of fertility, wealth, and prosperity. These facts are tremendously significant, for the return of Israel has occurred in our generation.

Ezekiel's prophecy obviously could not have been fulfilled prior to 1945, for the nation Israel was not regathered to their ancient land. Until our generation, Israel's situation did not correspond to that which is described in Ezekiel's passage. Ezekiel's prophecy of twenty-five hundred years ago seems to have anticipated the return of Israel to their ancient land as a prelude to the climax of this present age.

INVASION AFTER REBUILDING OF CITIES

Another important aspect of the prophecy is found in verse eleven where it states that the people of Israel will be dwelling "securely, all of them dwelling without walls, and having neither bars nor gates." It was customary in ancient times, whenever a city prospered, to build a wall around it. One can go to ancient lands and see the ruins of walls around most important cities. They would, at least, have a fortress with a wall around it to which they could retire if the houses themselves were scattered and a wall about the houses was impracticable. In other words, it was customary to build walls about cities. In our modern day, this custom has been discontinued for the obvious reason that a wall is no protection against modern warfare.

If one goes to Israel today, though one can see many fabulous cities being built and marvelous developments taking place, one will not find a single new city with a wall built around it. They are cities without walls. How did Ezekiel know that at a future time the war situation would be such that cities would be built without walls? Of course, the answer is a simple one. He was guided by the inspiration of God, and it was not a matter of his own wisdom. But in this scene he is describing a modern situation, something that could not and would not be true back in the days of old, before Christ. This detail is very important because un-walled villages point to Israel's situation today.

INVASION AT A TIME OF ISRAEL'S PROSPERITY

A third feature may also be observed. This portion of Scripture is explicit that one of the reasons why Russia wants to conquer the land of Israel is that it had become a land of great wealth. Russia comes to take a prey, to take silver and gold, and the wealth that has been accumulated (cp. Ezekiel 38:12, 13). Until our generation, the geographic area of the land of Israel was anything but something to be prized. It did not have any wealth; it was a land that was strewn with stones; a land that was backward as far as civilization is concerned. Many of the areas that at one time were fruitful in Bible times were unused prior to Israel's reclamation. The land was eroded and useless as far as agriculture is concerned.

Since the Israelites have gone back to their ancient land, they have done fabulous things. They have taken rocky fields, gathered the stones in piles along the edge, and cultivated and irrigated the ground and made it to bring forth abundantly. They have reclaimed swamps where mosquitoes and malaria made civilization impossible before. In fact, the first people that tried to do something about it lost their lives because of the unhealthy situation. These former swamps are today one of the richest areas of farm land in the entire world. It is almost incredible what has occurred there since

1948. They have spent money, they have put forth extreme effort, and from one end of Israel to the other tremendous progress is in evidence. The result is today that Israel is beginning once again to be a nation that has wealth. A great deal is being exported to other countries, and money is beginning to flow back to the little nation of Israel.

In addition to agricultural wealth, there are some factors that Ezekiel did not know which we know today. One factor is that to the east of the land of Israel are tremendous oil reserves. One of the largest and richest oil fields in the entire world is in the Middle East. It is outside the present geographic area of Israel, but the nation that wants to control that oil land must control the nation Israel. It is obvious that the tremendous oil reserves of the Middle East are one of the prizes that Russia wants to secure.

Another aspect of wealth which has come to light in modern times is the chemical value of the Dead Sea area, where water has evaporated for centuries, leaving its mineral deposit. Israel has established a plant at the south end of the Dead Sea and is reclaiming the chemicals. Millions of dollars of those chemicals are being shipped, and they have just begun to tap this wealth. Ezekiel anticipated the time when the land of Israel would be fabulously wealthy.

MILITARY IMPORTANCE OF ISRAEL

In addition to all these factors, it is obvious that the geographic location of the Middle East, being as it is a hub

between three major continents—Europe, Asia, and Africa—
is of tremendous strategic importance to any nation that
wants to dominate the world. The geographic significance
of the Middle East alone would be worth a real effort on
the part of Russia to have this portion of the world under its
control. Again Ezekiel anticipates today's situation.

THE DESTRUCTION OF THE INVADING ARMY

When the Russian army comes down upon this land they
are met with complete and utter destruction. Strange to say,
as we examine the Scriptures, we do not find them being
destroyed by an opposing army, but rather it seems to be
by divine intervention. Somehow God by His own power
destroys the army. In Ezekiel 38:19, 20 a description is given
of earthquakes, mountains falling, and other disturbances
which hinder their progress.

Then God declares:

And I will call for a sword against him unto all
my mountains, saith the Lord Jehovah: every
man's sword shall be against his brother. And with
pestilence and with blood will I enter into judgment
with him; and I will rain upon him, and upon his
hordes, and upon the many peoples that are with
him, an overflowing shower, and great hailstones,
fire, and brimstone. And I will magnify myself, and
sanctify myself, and I will make myself known in the

eyes of many nations; and they shall know that I am Jehovah (Ezekiel 38:21-23, ASV).

The army's destruction is portrayed in Ezekiel 39:4ff. God declares: "Thou shalt fall upon the mountains of Israel, thou, and all thy hordes, and the peoples that are with thee: I will give thee unto the ravenous birds of every sort, and to the beasts of the field to be devoured." In other words, the army is completely destroyed, and the means used are earthquakes, hailstones, fire and brimstone. It seems also that parts of the army begin to fight each other, so that every man's sword is against his brother.

Some natural questions are raised about this. Some have suggested that the description of hailstones, fire and brimstone might be Ezekiel's way of describing modern warfare, such as atomic warfare. There is a possibility that Ezekiel was using terms that he knew to describe a future situation for which he did not have a vocabulary. The language of Scripture indicates, however, that the victory over this invading horde is something that God does. It is God, Himself, who is destroying the army.

In any case, regardless of the means, the army is completely destroyed and chapter 39 goes on to describe the aftermath. For months thereafter they have the awful task of burying the dead. For a long period after that men are given full-time employment as additional bodies are discovered, and the process of burial continues. Attention is also directed to the debris of the battle. It is used as kindling wood for some seven years. The general character of this battle and its outcome seems to be quite clear, even though we may have some questions and problems about the details.

TIME OF THE INVASION

One of the principal questions one could ask about this battle is, When is the battle going to occur? It has not occurred in the past. What indication do we have in this portion of Scripture that the battle will occur at a specific time? Unfortunately, varying opinions have been offered by capable Bible scholars on this point, and there has been considerable disagreement. Some have felt that the battle will take place before the rapture, others believe it will take place in connection with the battle of Armageddon, or the battle of the Great Day of God Almighty, at the end of the great tribulation. Some place it at the beginning of the millennium, as an act of rebellion against Christ. Some find it at the end of the millennium, for there is a reference to Gog and Magog in Revelation 20. Others put it in the earlier part of Daniel's seventieth week, just before the great tribulation.

It will not be possible to consider all these views in detail, but there are some hints that provide a good clue as to when this battle will take place. One of the hints given is that the battle takes place at a time when Israel has been regathered into their ancient land, and are dwelling securely and at rest. There are not too many times when Israel is at rest in God's prophetic program. They have been scattered and persecuted over the face of the earth, and not even in the future will Israel have many periods of rest.

Certainly Israel is not at rest today. Israel is an armed camp, living under a truce with their Arab neighbors about them. Their enemies would drive every Israelite into the Mediterranean Sea and kill them if they could. The reason that they do not is because, humanly speaking, Israel has a good army which is more than a match for its neighbors. Today an armed truce and a no-man's land separate Israel from their enemy.

Every young Israeli man is required to have two and one-half years of military training and every young woman two years of military training. While the women are trained for jobs that are not necessarily of combatant type, they also learn to use weapons, so that if they need to fight, they can. After military training, many of them are settled in villages near the border, where they can serve a double purpose—following their occupation, whatever it is, and serving as guards for the border of Israel. Israel's state of unrest does not correspond to Ezekiel's prophecy. If Russia should invade the Middle East today, it would not be a fulfillment of this portion of Scripture. That has to take place when Israel is at rest.

One point at which Israel will be at rest is in the millennial kingdom. But we are told expressly that, in the millennial kingdom, there will be no war (Isaiah 2:4), and only when the rebellion occurs at the end of the millennium when Satan is let loose (Revelation 20:7-9) does war break out.

Certainly Israel is not going to be at rest under these circumstances either, once Satan is let loose.

Some have suggested that Israel will be at rest in the period of great tribulation, and that the prophecy of Russia will be fulfilled at that time. In the time of great tribulation, Israel will not be at rest, for Christ told them to flee to the mountains to escape their persecutors. Therefore the invasion described by Ezekiel could not be a part of the battle of Armageddon, or the battle of the Great Day of God Almighty.

There is only one period in the future that clearly fits this description of Ezekiel, and that is the first half of Daniel's seventieth week of God's program for Israel (Daniel 9:27). After the church has been raptured and saints have been raised from the dead and the living saints have been caught up to be with the Lord, a confederacy of nations will emerge in the Mediterranean Sea. Out of that confederacy will come a strong man who will become its dictator (discussed in previous chapters). He is described in Daniel 9:26 as "the prince that shall come." He will enter into a seven-year covenant of protection and peace with the people of Israel (Daniel 9:27).

Under that covenant, Israel will be able to relax, for their Gentile enemies will have become their friends, apparently guaranteed their borders and promised them freedom. During that first three and one-half years, we have the one time when regathered Israel is at rest and secure. Apparently Russia will invade the land of Israel during that period, possibly toward its close, and the Scripture will then be fulfilled.

PROBLEMS OF INTERPRETATION

There are some other problems in the passage which merit study. A reference is made to bows and arrows, to shields and chariots, and to swords. These, of course, are antiquated weapons from the standpoint of modern warfare. The large use of horses is understandable as Russia today uses horses a great deal in connection with their army. But why should they use armor, spears, bows and arrows? This certainly poses a problem.

There have been two or more answers given. One of them is this that Ezekiel is using language with which he was familiar—the weapons that were common in his day—to anticipate modern weapons. What he is saying is that when this army comes, it will be fully equipped with the weapons of war. Such an interpretation, too, has problems. We are told in the passage that they used the wooden shafts of the spears and the bow and arrows for kindling wood. If these are symbols, it would be difficult to burn symbols. However, even in modern warfare there is a good deal of wood used. Possibly this is the explanation. We are not in a position today to settle this problem with any finality.

A second solution is that the battle is preceded by a disarmament agreement between nations. If this were the case, it would be necessary to resort to primitive weapons easily and secretly made if a surprise attack were to be achieved. This would allow a literal interpretation of the passage.

A third solution has also been suggested based on the

premise that modern missile warfare will have developed in that day to the point where missiles will seek out any considerable amount of metal. Under these circumstances, it would be necessary to abandon the large use of metal weapons and substitute wood such as is indicated in the primitive weapons. Whatever the explanation, the most sensible interpretation is that the passage refers to actual weapons pressed into use because of the peculiar circumstances of that day.

THE FUTURE OF RUSSIA

The general character of the passage, the nature of the war, the invasion when it comes, and the outcome is, however, perfectly clear. What significance does it have to the modern scene? First of all, if we understand the passage correctly, Russia, instead of being a nation which is going to dominate the whole world, is headed for a tremendous military defeat. It is not possible to predict what is going to happen between now and the time this battle takes place, but the Bible seems quite clear that there is no room for a Russian-dominated world empire. The Bible prophesies only four world empires. The empire of the great tribulation period which will come as a form of the revived Roman Empire, is the final form of the fourth empire of Daniel, not a Russian Empire. This, in turn, will be succeeded by the millennial reign of Christ.

The passage seems to confirm that Russia, instead of becoming a world power that is going to dominate the whole world, is instead headed for an awful defeat, a judgment from

God because of its blasphemy and ungodliness. If this becomes true during the time of the seventieth week of Daniel, it may explain something that otherwise might be difficult.

THE EMERGENCE OF A WORLD EMPIRE

We know that in the last half of Daniel's seventieth week there will be a world government headed by the ruler of the Mediterranean confederacy. The question is, how does he forge this world empire so quickly and so easily, and apparently without fighting for it? We learn in Revelation 13:4 that the question is asked, "Who is able to make war with him?" i.e., with the Beast. The answer is that nobody is able to make war with him. It should be obvious that if Russia and her satellites are destroyed as military powers, the other side of the balance of power, represented by the Mediterranean confederacy, is then in a position to dominate the whole world. Nobody is able, for at least a time, to contest their right to rule.

The destruction of the Russian army may be the preface to the world government which will sweep the world during the last half of Daniel's seventieth week and be in power at the time Christ comes back to establish His millennial kingdom. These two portions of Scripture, while they concern themselves with a future war, are of tremendous significance as we face the present world scene and the dominance of Russia as a military power. We can trust that God, in due time, and perhaps sooner than we think, will bring these Scriptures to their sure conclusion and fulfillment.[1]

COMMON QUESTIONS RELATED TO RUSSIA, THE MIDDLE EAST, AND THE END OF DAYS

1. DOES THE BIBLE PREDICT A WAR BETWEEN THE UNITED STATES AND RUSSIA?

Just days before he died on the cross Jesus said that the end times will be punctuated by military conflict: "You will hear of wars and threats of wars, but don't panic. Yes, these things must take place, but the end won't follow immediately. Nation will go to war against nation, and kingdom against kingdom" (Matthew 24:6-7).

Since the United States and Russia are the two most powerful military machines in the world and have engaged in a seventy-year standoff, it's reasonable to wonder whether these two powers will come to blows in the future. Inquiring minds want to know.

We've seen in this book that Russia is referenced in Scripture in Ezekiel 38–39. Russia will be a part of the first main war of the end times—the War of Gog and Magog. America, on the other hand, is not mentioned in the Bible, at least explicitly.

All agree that the words *America* or *the United States* are absent from Scripture, but some believe they've discovered symbolic references to the US in three main texts: the unnamed nation in Isaiah 18:1-2, Babylon in Revelation 17–19, or "the merchants of Tarshish, with all the young lions" (KJV) in Ezekiel 38:13. One other view is that America is the ten lost tribes of Israel.

Ezekiel 38:13 and its reference to "the merchants of Tarshish, with all the young lions" (KJV) is the only one of the four views that could possibly refer to the United States. The others are tenuous at best.

The words "young lions" are employed in Scripture to refer to energetic rulers, so this could refer to leaders or the nations that have come out of Tarshish.[1]

Tarshish in Ezekiel's day was in the most distant western region of the known world. In Jonah 1:1-3, when God called the prophet Jonah to go east to preach to Nineveh, Jonah went as far as he could to the west, to Tarshish, a Phoenician colony likely in what today is Spain.

We discussed this briefly in chapter 4. The young lions and the merchants of Tarshish could be a reference to the lands that emerged from Spain, including the nations of South and Central America. Some contend that ancient Tarshish was actually in England. If this view is correct, the "young lions" could represent "the United States, Canada, Australia, New Zealand, and other present-day western democracies."[2] This would be a clear biblical reference to the role of America in the end times.

In any event, nothing in this passage refers to a war between the United States and Russia. Ezekiel 38:13 presents Tarshish and the young lions as sitting on the sidelines when Russia attacks Israel, not engaging in battle. So even if the merchants of Tarshish is a veiled reference to the United States, it points toward Russia and the US once again avoiding an all-out showdown of forces.

Russia and the United States may square off militarily at some point in the future, but the Bible doesn't speak to this issue one way or the other.

2. DOES THE BIBLE PREDICT THE USE OF NUCLEAR WEAPONS IN THE END TIMES?

The dawn of the nuclear age in the 1940s ushered in a staggering new reality—humanity's ability to blow up this planet. Since that time, fears have mounted that the world will end in a nuclear nightmare. This fear was palpable during the tense days of the Cold War. Anyone growing up in the 1950s through the 1970s remembers the tangible threat of nuclear war. Russia has the world's largest stockpile of nukes, followed closely by the United States. During the Cold War, the threat of a nuclear exchange was a sum-of-all-fears scenario.

In the last twenty years, the proliferation of nuclear weapons has changed everything. Pakistan, India, and China have nuclear weapons. North Korea and its bizarre leader have the bomb, and the world watches as Kim Jong-un conducts ballistic missile tests in an effort to obtain a missile that can deliver a nuclear payload to the United States. Terrorist states like Iran are waiting in the wings to join the nuclear club.

With this many nuclear players on the scene, and with Russia as the leader of the pack, many people want to know if the Bible predicts the use of nuclear weapons in the end times. In today's volatile international environment, it's reasonable to wonder whether the Bible addresses this critical question.

Three main biblical passages are cited in support of the view that a nuclear exchange is prophesied in the latter years:

> The LORD will send a plague on all the nations that fought against Jerusalem. Their people will become like walking corpses, their flesh rotting away. Their eyes will rot in their sockets, and their tongues will rot in their mouths.
>
> ZECHARIAH 14:12

> By the same word, the present heavens and earth have been stored up for fire. They are being kept for the day of judgment, when ungodly people will be destroyed. . . . But the day of the Lord will come as unexpectedly as a thief. Then the heavens will pass away with a terrible noise, and the very elements themselves will disappear in fire, and the earth and everything on it will be found to deserve judgment. . . . On that day, he will set the heavens on fire, and the elements will melt away in the flames.
>
> 2 PETER 3:7, 10, 12

The first angel blew his trumpet, and hail and fire mixed with blood were thrown down on the earth. One-third of the earth was set on fire, one-third of the trees were burned, and all the green grass was burned.

Then the second angel blew his trumpet, and a great mountain of fire was thrown into the sea. One-third of the water in the sea became blood, one-third of all things living in the sea died, and one-third of all the ships on the sea were destroyed.

Then the third angel blew his trumpet, and a great star fell from the sky, burning like a torch. It fell on one-third of the rivers and on the springs of water. The name of the star was Bitterness. It made one-third of the water bitter, and many people died from drinking the bitter water.

Then the fourth angel blew his trumpet, and one-third of the sun was struck, and one-third of the moon, and one-third of the stars, and they became dark. And one-third of the day was dark, and also one-third of the night.

REVELATION 8:7-12

Each of these passages describes devastating destruction. Revelation 8 even mentions objects falling from the sky that contaminate the planet, much like a nuclear explosion would.

In each of these passages I believe the context is clear that the destruction comes from the hand of God, not nuclear detonation. Even in Revelation 8, the ecological disasters are explicitly traced to God as the source of these judgments, not some madman. The seven seal judgments in Revelation 6 are opened and unleashed by Jesus, and the seventh seal judgment in Revelation 8:1 contains the seven trumpets. Therefore, it follows that the trumpets are also divine judgments. This point is further strengthened in that the trumpet judgments are very similar to the Egyptian plagues in the book of Exodus. They are even called plagues in Revelation 9:20. The Egyptian plagues were not natural occurrences or man-made; they were direct judgments from God.

Nuclear weapons may be used in the near future or during the end times. As weapons of mass destruction mushroom, it's difficult to see how they can be kept out of the hands of unstable leaders or terrorists. However, I don't believe the Bible says anything about nuclear weapons. When the Bible is silent, we're wise not to go beyond what's written.

3. DOES THE BIBLE PREDICT THE DESTRUCTION OF SYRIA IN THE END TIMES?

Since the founding of the modern state of Israel in 1948, Syria has remained an entrenched enemy of Israel. The two nations have faced off in three bloody wars: the War of Independence (1948), the Six-Day War (1967), and the Yom Kippur War (1973). The loss of the Golan Heights to Israel in 1973 was a major blow to the Syrians.

Since early 2011, and the outbreak of civil war, Syria

has been a major international flash point. The brutality of Bashar al-Assad has been on full display for the world to see. More than four hundred thousand Syrians have died in the bloody civil war. Russia and Iran have propped up the Assad regime, sending troops and air power. For Iran, Syria is part of the strategy for a "Shiite full moon" across the region. For Russia, presence in Syria expands Russian influence, and many believe Russia is using the chaos to flood Europe with refugees, further stretching and weakening European financial resources and increasing the threat of terror in Europe.

About five million Syrian refugees have fled the country, and more than six million within the nation have been displaced. Most Syrian refugees have relocated in the Middle East, but more than half a million have come to the shores of European nations. With mounting deaths and displacement, the Syrian refugee crisis has been called "the worst human security disaster of the twenty-first century."[3]

Added to all this misery, ISIS has focused much of its effort in Syria primarily because Dabiq, Syria, "is where the Prophet Mohammed is supposed to have predicted that the armies of Islam and 'Rome' would meet for the final battle that will precede the end of time and the triumph of true Islam."[4]

Questions about Syria are closely related to Russia because the chaos in Syria has afforded Russia a unique opportunity to accomplish many of its goals and has brought Russia, Iran, and Turkey into closer alliance.

With all these factors converging in Syria, many prophecy

teachers believe the world focus on Syria in the last few years points toward the fulfillment of Isaiah 17 in the near future. Isaiah 17:1-2 prophesies the destruction of Damascus, Syria's capital: "Look, the city of Damascus will disappear! It will become a heap of ruins. The towns of Aroer will be deserted. Flocks will graze in the streets and lie down undisturbed, with no one to chase them away."

Many who believe the fulfillment of this prophecy is imminent hold that Israel will take out Damascus, possibly by a nuclear attack, while others believe the destruction will be supernatural. Often only the first two verses of Isaiah 17 are quoted, yet if we continue reading the passage, we find it also predicts the destruction of northern Israel at the same time. In Isaiah's day, Ephraim was the name for the Northern Kingdom of Israel. Notice that at the same time Damascus is destroyed, Israel is too:

> "The fortified towns of Israel [NASB, "Ephraim"] will
>   also be destroyed,
>   and the royal power of Damascus will end.
> All that remains of Syria
>   will share the fate of Israel's departed glory,"
>   declares the LORD of Heaven's Armies.
>
> "In that day Israel's glory will grow dim;
>   its robust body will waste away.
> The whole land will look like a grainfield
>   after the harvesters have gathered the grain.

It will be desolate,
    like the fields in the valley of Rephaim after the
      harvest.
Only a few of its people will be left,
    like stray olives left on a tree after the harvest.
Only two or three remain in the highest branches,
    four or five scattered here and there on the limbs,"
declares the LORD, the God of Israel.

Then at last the people will look to their Creator
    and turn their eyes to the Holy One of Israel.
They will no longer look to their idols for help
    or worship what their own hands have made.

ISAIAH 17:3-8

In light of the overall context of Isaiah 17, I believe the best interpretation sees the fulfillment of this passage in the eighth century BC, when both Damascus, the capital of Syria (732 BC), and Samaria, the capital of Israel (722 BC), were pounded by the Assyrians. In the Assyrian invasion of Syria and Israel, there's a clear point in time when both Damascus and Samaria were destroyed, just as Isaiah 17 predicts.

The past fulfillment of Isaiah 17 finds further confirmation in Isaiah 17:12-14, which was fulfilled in 701 BC, when 185,000 Assyrians under the command of Sennacherib were destroyed in one night by God (see Isaiah 37:36-38).

As the fuse on the Middle East powder keg continues to burn, Syria, although not specifically singled out in Scripture, seems to be a key player in setting the stage. The chaos in Syria has created the vacuum for Russia and Iran to fill. Their presence in Syria on Israel's northern border foreshadows the future invasion of Israel by these nations and their allies in Ezekiel 38.

4. WHY IS IT TAKING SO LONG FOR JESUS TO RETURN?

Three times in the final chapter of the New Testament, Jesus promises to come back "soon" or "quickly" (see Revelation 22:7, 12, 20). As early as about thirty years after the death, resurrection, and ascension of Jesus, people were beginning to question and even mock the truth of Christ's return because it had not happened. The promise of his soon coming seemed to be fading away. They mistakenly believed that the delay of his coming equaled nonfulfillment. The apostle Peter challenged these first-century mockers and their erroneous thinking:

> Most importantly, I want to remind you that in the last days scoffers will come, mocking the truth and following their own desires. They will say, "What happened to the promise that Jesus is coming again? From before the times of our ancestors, everything has remained the same since the world was first created."
>
> 2 PETER 3:3-4

If people within three decades of Christ's ascension were wondering why it was taking so long for Jesus to return, then certainly people must be wondering the same thing almost two thousand years later.

A general answer to this question is found in the first coming of Jesus. God had a perfect time for his Son to come to earth the first time. Galatians 4:4 says, "But when the right time came, God sent his Son, born of a woman, subject to the law." The world stage was perfectly arranged for the coming of Jesus and the spread of the gospel: the Roman peace (*Pax Romana*) had brought relative stability to the world, Greek was a common language for the writing of the New Testament, and the Roman road system was a powerful means for taking the gospel all over the world of that day.

In the same way, we can rest assured that a sovereign God has a perfect time, known only to him, for the return of his Son. The Bible is clear that "God keeps his own calendar."[5]

More specifically, while we don't know every reason behind God's timing, he has told us at least two reasons for this apparent delay in his coming in 2 Peter 3:8-15. First, "God's calendar is a *heavenly* calendar."[6] As we read in 2 Peter 3:8, "You must not forget this one thing, dear friends: A day is like a thousand years to the Lord, and a thousand years is like a day." This refers to God's relationship to time. God views time differently than we do. "God's 'delay' is not really a delay at all in the dimensions of his existence. . . . We see the movement of time as a sequential series of still frames, passing one-by-one, as in a motion picture, but God sees the entire movement at once."[8]

D. Edmond Hiebert explains: "The point is not that time

has no meaning for God but rather that His use of time is extensive, so that He may use a thousand years to do what we might feel should be done in a day, as well as intensive, doing in a day what we might feel could only be done in a thousand years."[8] One way to understand the passage of time before Christ's coming is God's heavenly calendar, viewing time from his vantage point.

Second, "God's calendar is an *evangelistic* calendar."[8] This deals with God's use of time. Second Peter 3:9, 15 says, "The Lord isn't really being slow about his promise, as some people think. No, he is being patient for your sake. He does not want anyone to be destroyed, but wants everyone to repent. . . . And remember, our Lord's patience gives people time to be saved."

The extended time between Christ's two comings serves a redemptive purpose and underscores the patience and long-suffering of God. "God guides all human history as salvation history, moving nations and people groups to meet the appointments for redemption made for those who will hear the gospel and receive the Savior."[9] The "slowness" in Christ's coming is not the result of divine indifference, powerlessness, or distraction, but rather the gracious patience of God toward sinners in need of salvation.

Michael Green says, "It is not slowness but patience that delays the consummation of all history, and holds open the door to repentant sinners, even repentant scoffers. Not impotence but mercy is the reason for God's delay."[10] The character of God moves him to patiently wait to send his Son.

Since one of the reasons for the apparent delay of Christ's coming is God's mercy for sinners, believers should be alert to opportunities God gives us to be part of the "hastening" of his coming by sharing the Good News with those around us. Rather than wondering or worrying about the delay, may we be moved by God to keep working in light of his mercy and patience.

Notes

CHAPTER 1: THERE IS A BEAR IN THE WOODS

1. "Vladimir Putin," *Forbes*, accessed May 5, 2017, https://www.forbes.com /profile/vladimir-putin/.
2. "Putin Deplores Collapse of USSR," *BBC News*, April 25, 2005, http:// news.bbc.co.uk/2/hi/4480745.stm.
3. Pavlo Klimkin, "Putin's Desire for a New Russian Empire Won't Stop with Ukraine," *Guardian*, March 25, 2017, https://www.theguardian.com /commentisfree/2017/mar/25/putin-new-russian-empire-ukraine.
4. Jana Bakunina, "In Russia, Stalin Is Back," *NewStatesman*, October 6, 2015, http://www.newstatesman.com/world/europe/2015/10/russia -stalin-back.
5. Jonathan Adelman, "Thinking the Unthinkable: Russia Has Re-Emerged as a Great Power," *Huffington Post*, April 19, 2016, http://www .huffingtonpost.com/jonathan-adelman/thinking-the-unthinkable -_2_b_9720304.html.
6. Allan C. Brownfeld, "The Putin-Trump Alliance Threatens Europe, America," *Communities Digital News*, March 5, 2017, http://www .commdiginews.com/politics-2/the-putin-trump-alliance-threatens -europe-america-84910/.
7. Olivier Knox, "Defense Secretary Pick Mattis Calls Russia Top Threat, Says Iran Deal Will Be Enforced," Yahoo News, January 12, 2017, https:// www.yahoo.com/news/defense-secretary-pick-mattis-says-russia-top -threat-will-enforce-iran-deal-185357939.html; Paul Karp, "Vladimir

Putin Is a Bigger Threat than ISIS, John McCain Says," *The Guardian*, May 29, 2017, http://www.theguardian.com/us-news/2017/may/29/vladimir-putin-is-bigger-threat-than-isis-john-mccain-says.

8. Only nine nations are believed to currently have nuclear weapons. Russia has the world's largest stockpile of nuclear warheads (7,300), followed by the US (around 7,000). Russia and the US hold 90 percent of the world's nuclear arms. The rest of the world's nuclear powers are as follows: France (300), China (260), Britain (215), India (130), Pakistan (120), Israel (80), North Korea (fewer than 10). Kiersten Schmidt and Bill Marsh, "Which Countries Have Nuclear Weapons and How Big Their Arsenals Are," *New York Times*, December 23, 2016, https://www.nytimes.com/interactive/2016/12/23/world/nuclear-weapon-countries.html.

9. Fareed Zakaria writes, "Russia is the largest country on the planet—48 times larger than Germany and encompassing 11 time zones that straddle Europe, Asia, and the Middle East." Fareed Zakaria, "Why Putin Is World's Most Powerful Man," *CNN*, March 14, 2017, http://www.cnn.com/2017/03/13/opinions/putin-most-powerful-man-world-zakaria/.

10. Jeff Stone, "Meet Fancy Bear and Cozy Bear, Russian Groups Blamed for DNC Hack," *Christian Science Monitor*, June 15, 2016, http://www.csmonitor.com/World/Passcode/2016/0615/Meet-Fancy-Bear-and-Cozy-Bear-Russian-groups-blamed-for-DNC-hack.

11. Evan Osnos, David Remnick, and Joshua Yaffa, "Trump, Putin, and the New Cold War," *New Yorker*, March 6, 2017, http://www.newyorker.com/magazine/2017/03/06/trump-putin-and-the-new-cold-war.

12. Ibid.

13. Ibid.

14. David Ignatius, "Russia May Be Wounded, but It Can Still Bite," *Washington Post*, November 3, 2016, https://www.washingtonpost.com/opinions/russia-may-be-wounded-but-it-can-still-bite/2016/11/03/ec2287c0-a205-11e6-a44d-cc2898cfab06_story.html?tid=a_inl&utm_term=.1114581528bb.

15. Osnos, Remnick, and Yaffa, "Trump, Putin, and the New Cold War."

16. W. J. Hennigan and Tracy Wilkinson, "Scientists Move Doomsday Clock Closer to 'Midnight.' Trump's Comments on Nuclear Weapons Are a Big Reason Why," *Los Angeles Times*, January 26, 2017, http://www.latimes.com/politics/la-na-pol-trump-nuclear-weapons-20170126-story.html.

17. "Shock Poll: Startling Numbers of Americans Believe World Now in the

'End Times,'" Religion News Service, September 11, 2013, http://
religionnews.com/2013/09/11/shock-poll-startling-numbers-of-americans
-believe-world-now-in-the-end-times/.

18. "Public Sees a Future Full of Promise and Peril," Pew Research Center,
June 22, 2010, http://www.people-press.org/2010/06/22/public-sees
-a-future-full-of-promise-and-peril.

19. Jeff Brumley, "Global Events, Prophecy Stir Talk of 'End Times' Beliefs,"
Florida Times-Union, July 16, 2010, http://jacksonville.com/news
/metro/2010-07-16/story/global-events-prophecy-stir-talk-end
-times-beliefs.

20. Douglas Todd, "We Need to Bring End-Times Beliefs Out of Their Closet,"
Vancouver Sun, November 8, 2008, www.canada.com/vancouversun/news
/editorial/story.html?id=ac308456-5493-4756-8ad6-68d.

21. Walter Einenkel, "New Survey Shows That about 80% of Evangelicals
Believe the 'End Times' Are Near," *Daily Kos*, December 7, 2015, http://
www.dailykos.com/story/2015/12/7/1457887/-New-survey-shows-that
-about-80-of-Evangelicals-believe-the-end-times-are-near.

22. Jeremy Weber, "Survey Surprise: Many Americans See Syria as Sign of
Bible's End Times," *Christianity Today*, September 13, 2013, http://www
.christianitytoday.com/gleanings/2013/september/syria-survey-end-times
-armageddon-lifeway.html.

23. David Jeremiah, *Is This the End? Signs of God's Providence in a Disturbing
New World* (Nashville: W Publishing Group, 2016), 221.

24. Charles Dyer and Mark Tobey, *Clash of Kingdoms: What the Bible Says
about Russia, ISIS, Iran, and the End Times* (Nashville: Nelson Books,
2017), 61–62.

CHAPTER 2: THE FINAL GAME OF THRONES

1. J. Dwight Pentecost, *Things to Come: A Study in Biblical Eschatology*
(Grand Rapids, MI: Zondervan, 1964), 332.

2. Revelation 13:1 calls the Antichrist the "beast rising up out of the sea,"
which pictures the Gentile nations—see Revelation 17:15.

3. Revelation 6:1-2 describes the Antichrist as a rider on a white horse—a false
messiah—who brings a brief window of peace to the earth. We know he
brings peace because the next rider (in Revelation 6:3-4) destroys that peace.

4. Some today believe the Antichrist will be a Muslim, possibly even the
Islamic Mahdi, but 2 Thessalonians 2:4 says the Antichrist will declare

himself to be God. The central tenet of Islam is that there is one god, who is Allah. No practicing Muslim could take this step. The Islamic Mahdi could never do this.

5. Pentecost, *Things to Come*, 331–32.

6. John F. Walvoord, *The Nations in Prophecy* (Grand Rapids, MI: Zondervan, 1967), 139, 141.

7. In the previous verses (Revelation 9:1-12) a demonic invasion is described, so taking the army in Revelation 9:13-21 in the same light is consistent. Also, the way the army is described fits the demonic view. "Fire and smoke and burning sulfur" (Revelation 9:17) are associated with hell in the book of Revelation.

8. Charles C. Ryrie, *The Best Is Yet to Come* (Chicago: Moody Press, 1981), 69.

9. Vernon Grounds, "Jesus Is Going to Win," *Morning Glory*, January 4, 1994, 9, https://bible.org/illustration/jesus-going-win.

CHAPTER 3: IS RUSSIA REALLY IN THE BIBLE?

1. Reagan said this when he was governor of California. See Joel C. Rosenberg, "Ronald Reagan & Book of Ezekiel," IOM America Resources, July 11, 2011, http://archive.constantcontact.com/fs086/1101261534859 /archive/1106145003521.html.

2. Douglas Stuart, for example, claims Ezekiel 38–39 is widely misinterpreted. He says, "Many people who know little about how apocalyptic prophecy is properly interpreted have tried to equate Gog with some modern 'northern' nation. . . . No modern nation is mentioned in the Bible. . . . The history of any particular modern nation is not a subject that God has chosen to cause to be incorporated into His Word." Douglas Stuart, *Ezekiel*, Mastering the Old Testament, gen. ed. Lloyd J. Ogilvie, vol. 18 (Dallas: Word Publishing, 1988), 351. Stuart doesn't take any of the nations in Ezekiel 38 literally, but he does take all the nations in Ezekiel 25–32 literally. He makes the distinction based on his designation of Ezekiel 38–39 as "apocalyptic." Yet there is nothing in the text that indicates the places in Ezekiel 38 are to be taken in any way other than literally. I agree that modern nations aren't mentioned per se in Scripture; however, I believe that the places in Ezekiel 38 are ancient locations that represent the nations in the end times that will reside in those places.

3. Gog is mentioned before Magog, but Gog is the leader of this invasion. We will discuss the meaning of Gog in the next chapter.

4. Daniel I. Block, *The Book of Ezekiel, Chapters 25–48*, The New International Commentary on the Old Testament, gen. ed. R. K. Harrison and Robert L. Hubbard Jr. (Grand Rapids, MI: Eerdmans, 1998), 433.

5. Josephus, *Antiquities*, 1.6.1. Block places Magog in ancient Lydia in western Anatolia (modern Turkey). Block, *Book of Ezekiel*, 434.

6. *The Nelson Study Bible* (Nashville: Thomas Nelson, 1997), 1396, note on Ezekiel 38:2.

7. Charles C. Ryrie, *Ryrie Study Bible* (Chicago: Moody, 1995), 1323, note on Ezekiel 38:2. See also Mark Rooker, *Ezekiel*, Holman Old Testament Commentary, gen. ed. Max Anders (Nashville: B&H, 2005), 271.

8. Arnold G. Fruchtenbaum, *The Footsteps of the Messiah: A Study of the Sequence of Prophetic Events*, rev. ed. (Tustin, CA: Ariel Ministries, 2003), 107.

9. John MacArthur Jr., *The Future of Israel: Study Notes, Daniel 9:20–12:13* (Panorama City, CA: Word of Grace Communications, 1985), 78.

10. C. I. Scofield, ed., *The Scofield Reference Bible: The Holy Bible, Containing the Old and New Testaments* (New York: Oxford University Press, 1909), 883.

11. C. F. Keil, *Ezekiel, Daniel, Commentary on the Old Testament*, trans. James Martin, repr. (Grand Rapids, MI: Eerdmans, 1982), 159. Wilhelm Gesenius, *Gesenius' Hebrew and Chaldee Lexicon to the Old Testament Scriptures*, repr. (Grand Rapids, MI: Eerdmans, 1949), 752.

12. G. A. Cooke, *A Critical and Exegetical Commentary on the Book of Ezekiel*, ed. S. R. Driver, A. Plummer, and C. A. Briggs, The International Critical Commentary (Edinburgh: T & T Clark, 1936), 408–9.

13. John B. Taylor, *Ezekiel: An Introduction & Commentary*, Tyndale Old Testament Commentaries, gen. ed. D. J. Wiseman (Downers Grove, IL: InterVarsity, 1969), 244. For a comprehensive look at the evidence for Rosh as a place-name, see James D. Price "Rosh: An Ancient Land Known to Ezekiel," *Grace Theological Journal* 6 (1985): 67–89.

14. The mistranslation of *rosh* in many modern translations as an adjective can be traced to the Latin Vulgate of Jerome. Clyde E. Billington Jr., "The Rosh People in History and Prophecy (Part Two)" *Michigan Theological Journal* 3, no. 2 (Fall 1992): 54–61.

15. Block, *Book of Ezekiel*, 434.

16. Keil, *Ezekiel, Daniel*, 159.

17. Gesenius, *Gesenius' Hebrew and Chaldee Lexicon*, 752.

18. Joel C. Rosenberg, *Epicenter: Why the Current Rumblings in the Middle East Will Change Your Future*, rev. ed. (Carol Stream, IL: Tyndale, 2008), 86.

19. Billington, "The Rosh People (Part Two)," 145–46; Clyde E. Billington Jr., "The Rosh People in History and Prophecy (Part Three)," *Michigan Theological Journal* 4, no. 1 (Spring 1993): 59, 61; James D. Price, "Rosh: An Ancient Land Known to Ezekiel," *Grace Theological Journal* 6, no. 1 (1985): 71–73; Jon Mark Ruthven, *The Prophecy That Is Shaping History: New Research on Ezekiel's Vision of the End* (Fairfax, VA: Xulon Press, 2003). Thomas Ice writes, "It is very likely that the name Rosh is actually derived from the name Tiras in Genesis 10:2 in the Table of Nations. Billington notes the Akkadian tendency to drop or to change an initial 't' sound in a name especially if the initial 't' was followed by an 'r' sound. If you drop the initial 'T' from Tiras you are left with 'ras.'" Thomas Ice, "Ezekiel 38 and 39: Part IV," Pre-Trib Research Center, accessed May 25, 2017, http://www.pre-trib.org/data/pdf/Ice-(Part4) Ezekiel38&39.pdf. See also Billington, "The Rosh People (Part Two)," 166–67.

20. Billington, "The Rosh People (Part Two)," 145–46.

21. It is found three times in the Septuagint (LXX), ten times in Sargon's inscriptions, once in Assurbanipal's cylinder, once in Sennacherib's annals, and five times in Ugaritic tablets. See Price, "Rosh: An Ancient Land," 71–73.

22. Billington, "The Rosh People (Part Three)," 48, 59, 61.

23. Fruchtenbaum, *Footsteps of the Messiah*, 108–9.

24. Daniel 11:40 mentions an end-time figure called the "king of the north" who will contest and challenge the authority of the final Antichrist. Because of the focus on the north in Daniel 11:40 and Ezekiel 38, John MacArthur holds that the king of the north in Daniel 11:40 is a reference to Russia and is a parallel passage to Ezekiel 38. MacArthur, *Future of Israel*, 78–79. Leon Wood also identifies the king of the north in Daniel 11:40 as Russia. See Leon Wood, *A Commentary on Daniel* (Eugene, OR: Wipf and Stock, 1998), 308–10. David Jeremiah similarly believes Daniel 11:40 "meshes perfectly" with Ezekiel's prophecy. David Jeremiah, *Is This the End? Signs of God's Providence in a Disturbing New World* (Nashville: W Publishing Group, 2016), 213.

25. John F. Walvoord, *The Nations in Prophecy* (Grand Rapids, MI: Zondervan, 1967), 106.

26. Paul P. Enns, ed., *Shepherd's Notes: Ezekiel* (Nashville: B&H, 1998), 92.

27. Walter C. Kaiser Jr., *Preaching and Teaching the Last Things: Old Testament Eschatology for the Life of the Church* (Grand Rapids, MI: Baker Academic, 2011), 92. Kaiser also believes Russia will lead the alliance of nations, referring to it as the "Russian-Iranian horde" and "Russian-Iranian coalition (93, 95).

28. Charles Dyer and Mark Tobey, *Clash of Kingdoms: What the Bible Says about Russia, ISIS, Iran, and the End Times* (Nashville: Nelson Books, 2017), 16.

29. Charles H. Dyer, "Ezekiel," in *The Bible Knowledge Commentary*, ed. John F. Walvoord and Roy B. Zuck (Wheaton, IL: Victor Books, 1985), 1300.

30. Lamar Eugene Cooper, Sr., *Ezekiel*, The New American Commentary, vol. 17 (Nashville: B&H, 1994), 331.

31. Charles C. Ryrie, *The Best Is Yet to Come* (Chicago: Moody, 1981), 55.

32. Jeremiah, *Is This the End?*, 211.

33. J. Vernon McGee, *How Russia Will Be Destroyed: Ezekiel 38-39* (Pasadena, CA: Thru the Bible Radio Network, n.d.), 3.

34. J. Dwight Pentecost, *Things to Come: A Study in Biblical Eschatology* (Grand Rapids, MI: Zondervan, 1964), 328.

35. Rosenberg, *Epicenter*, 82, 87.

36. See, for example, Hank Hanegraaff, *Has God Spoken? Memorable Proofs of the Bible's Divine Inspiration* (Nashville: Thomas Nelson, 2011), 236.

37. Matthew Henry, "Complete Commentary on Ezekiel 38:4," *Matthew Henry's Complete Commentary on the Whole Bible* (1706), StudyLight.org, accessed June 8, 2017, http://www.studylight.org/commentaries/mhm /ezekiel-38.html.

38. Patrick Fairbairn, "The Assault of Gog and His Destruction" in *Ezekiel and the Book of His Prophecy: An Exposition.*

39. Robert Jamieson, A. R. Fausset, and David Brown, *Jamieson, Fausset & Brown's Commentary on the Whole Bible*, Zondervan Classic Reference Series (originally published as *Commentary Critical and Explanatory on the Whole Bible*, 1871), repr. (Grand Rapids, MI: Zondervan, 1961), 721.

40. William Kelly, *Notes on Ezekiel* (London: George Morrish, 1876), 195.

41. Ibid., 191, 194.

42. Arno Clemens Gaebelein, "Commentary on Ezekiel 38:4," *Gaebelein's Annotated Bible*, StudyLight.org, accessed June 8, 2017, http://www.studylight.org/commentaries/gab/ezekiel-38.html.

CHAPTER 4: EZEKIEL'S PROPHETIC INTELLIGENCE BRIEFING

1. Joel C. Rosenberg, *Epicenter: Why the Current Rumblings in the Middle East Will Change Your Future*, rev. ed. (Carol Stream, IL: Tyndale, 2008), 104.

2. Christopher J. H. Wright, *The Message of Ezekiel: A New Heart and a New Spirit*, The Bible Speaks Today, ed. J. A. Motyer (Downers Grove, IL: InterVarsity, 2001), 324–26. Eckhard Schnabel rejects a literal interpretation of Ezekiel 38–39 and cautions against pressing the details too far. He believes Ezekiel 38 is "a symbolic vision of God's ultimate victory over the enemies of his people." He adds, "It seems plausible . . . to interpret the Gog prophecy as Ezekiel's vision of the radicalized conflict between Yahweh and the nations in which Yahweh wins the final victory over the cosmic forces of chaos (represented by Gog and his allies)." Eckhard Schnabel, *40 Questions about the End Times*, ed. Benjamin L. Merkle (Grand Rapids, MI: Kregel, 2011), 224. If this view is correct, why does Ezekiel list ten specific names and give all the details he provides? I believe a symbolic interpretation fails to give due weight to all the intricate details of Ezekiel's prophecy. The symbolic view also goes against the literal fulfillment of hundreds of Old Testament prophecies (see, for example, Isaiah 7:14; 44:28–45:7; Micah 5:2). Biblical prophecies have been literally fulfilled, and this is true even in the book of Ezekiel. The prophecies in Ezekiel 4–24 concerning the coming destruction of Jerusalem were literally fulfilled. The regathering of the Jewish people in Ezekiel 37 is in the process of being fulfilled. It began in 1948. If the prophecies in Ezekiel 4–37 have been literally fulfilled, why should we interpret Ezekiel 38–39 symbolically?

3. Charles Lee Feinberg, *The Prophecy of Ezekiel: The Glory of the Lord* (Eugene, OR: Wipf and Stock, 2003), 219.

4. Charles Dyer and Mark Tobey, *Clash of Kingdoms: What the Bible Says about Russia, ISIS, Iran, and the End Times* (Nashville: Nelson Books, 2017), 21.

5. Paul P. Enns, ed., *Shepherd's Notes: Ezekiel* (Nashville: B&H, 1998), 92.

6. Charles C. Ryrie, *Ryrie Study Bible* (Chicago: Moody Press, 1995), 1323, note on Ezekiel 38:2. See also Mark Rooker, *Ezekiel*, Holman Old Testament Commentary, gen. ed. Max Anders (Nashville: B&H, 2005), 271.

7. C. I. Scofield, *Scofield Reference Notes* (1917 edition), note to Ezekiel 38:2, Bible Study Tools, accessed June 8, 2017, http://www.biblestudytools.com /commentaries/scofield-reference-notes/ezekiel/ezekiel-38.html.

8. Arnold G. Fruchtenbaum, *The Footsteps of the Messiah: A Study of the*

Sequence of Prophetic Events, rev. ed. (Tustin, CA: Ariel Ministries, 2003), 108.

9. John Phillips, *Exploring the Future: A Comprehensive Guide to Bible Prophecy*, 3rd ed. (Grand Rapids, MI: Kregel, 2003), 327.

10. Josephus, *Antiquities*, 1.6.1.

11. Walter C. Kaiser Jr., *Preaching and Teaching the Last Things: Old Testament Eschatology for the Life of the Church* (Grand Rapids, MI: Baker Academic, 2011), 92.

12. Lamine Ghanmi, "Russia Enlarges Military Footprint in Libya," UPI, March 20, 2017, http://www.upi.com/Top_News/Voices/2017/03/20 /Russia-enlarges-military-footprint-in-Libya/6031490019941/.

13. Darius Shahtahmasebi, "Russia Eyes Libya," *Anti-Media*, March 27, 2017, http://theantimedia.org/russia-libya-putin-middle-east/.

14. Thomas Constable, "Commentary on Ezekiel 38:4: Expository Notes of Dr. Thomas Constable," StudyLight.org, accessed June 8, 2017, http:// www.studylight.org/commentaries/dcc/ezekiel-38.html#1.

15. See the New American Standard Bible.

16. See the discussion on the timing of the War of Gog and Magog in chapter 8.

17. Kaiser, *Preaching and Teaching*, 92.

18. Rosenberg, *Epicenter*, 130.

19. Not all commentators agree that Daniel 11:40 and Ezekiel 38–39 are parallel. John Walvoord rejects equating these two texts. He believes Daniel describes a war that occurs "possibly several years after the battle described in Ezekiel." John F. Walvoord, *Daniel*, ed. Philip E. Rawley and Charles H. Dyer, rev. ed. (Chicago: Moody, 2012), 355. Some Bible translations—the New Living Translation among them—seem closed to this possibility, but others (like the New American Standard Bible) seem to invite the comparison. The best defense I've seen for equating Daniel 11:40 and Ezekiel 38–39 is from Leon Wood in his commentary on Daniel. He provides five excellent arguments in support of his position. See Leon Wood, *A Commentary on Daniel* (Eugene, OR: Wipf and Stock, 1998), 309–10. See also Mark Hitchcock, "The King of the North in Daniel 11:40" (ThM thesis, Dallas Theological Seminary, 1991).

20. The full quote is "No war without Egypt, no peace without Syria." Quoted in Michael J. Totten, "No Peace without Syria," *Commentary*, August 31, 2009, https://www.commentarymagazine.com/foreign-policy/middle-east /no-peace-without-syria/.

21. Kaiser, *Preaching and Teaching*, 92. Joel Rosenberg supports this view. See Rosenberg, *Epicenter*, 130.

22. Saudi Arabia does harbor some terrorist elements but is vehemently opposed to Iran. Yemen is engrossed in a vicious civil war pitting the government against Houthi rebels backed by Iran.

23. Fruchtenbaum, *Footsteps of the Messiah*, 111.

24. Ibid., 112.

25. Rosenberg, *Epicenter*, 138.

CHAPTER 5: TRIPLE THREAT: RUSSIA, IRAN, AND TURKEY

1. "Kremlin: U.S. Has 'Emotional Obsession' with Russia," CNN, May 12, 2017, http://www.cnn.com/videos/tv/2017/05/12/lead-chance -kremlin-accuses-u-s-of-being-obsessed-with-russia-live.cnn, 2:59.

2. Abedin Taherkenareh, "Why Russia, Turkey and Iran Are Natural Allies," *The Conversation*, January 5, 2017, http://theconversation.com/why -russia-turkey-and-iran-are-natural-allies-70819.

3. Christian Caryl, "Sorry, but Putin's Still Winning," *Washington Post*, May 12, 2017, https://www.washingtonpost.com/news/democracy-post /wp/2017/05/12/sorry-but-putins-still-winning/?utm_term =.44f169d699a4.

4. Neil MacFarquhar and David E. Sanger, "Russia Sends Bombers to Syria Using Base in Iran," *New York Times*, August 16, 2016, https://www .nytimes.com/2016/08/17/world/middleeast/russia-iran-base-syria.html.

5. John Bacon, "Putin Meets with Iranian Leader, Touts 'Reliable and Stable Partner,'" *USA Today*, March 28, 2017, http://www.usatoday.com/story /news/world/2017/03/28/putin-meets-iranian-leader-touts-reliable-and -stable-partner/99723886/.

6. Ibid.

7. Douglas E. Schoen with Evan Roth Smith, *Putin's Master Plan: To Destroy Europe, Divide NATO, and Restore Russian Power and Global Influence* (New York: Encounter Books, 2016), 84.

8. Ahmad Majidyar, "Iran-Controlled Militant Group Says Regional Alliance Will Create 'Shiite Full Moon,'" Middle East Institute, May 11, 2017, http://www.mideasti.org/content/io/iran-controlled-militant-group-says -regional-alliance-will-create-shiite-full-moon.

9. Martin Chulov, "Amid Syrian Chaos, Iran's Game Plan Emerges: A Path to

the Mediterranean," *Guardian*, October 8, 2016, https://www.theguardian.com/world/2016/oct/08/iran-iraq-syria-isis-land-corridor.

10. Majidyar, "Iran-Controlled Militant Group."

11. Chulov, "Iran's Game Plan Emerges."

12. Karim El-Bar, "Proxies and Politics: Why Iran Funds Foreign Militias," *Middle East Eye*, October 6, 2016, http://www.middleeasteye.net/essays/proxies-and-politics-why-iran-funds-foreign-militias-2124504867.

13. Alireza Nader, "Iran at Putin's Mercy," *National Interest*, January 12, 2017, http://nationalinterest.org/blog/the-buzz/iran-putins-mercy-19035.

14. "Iran Threatens 'Death to Israel' at Military Parade," *Tower*, April 19, 2017, http://www.thetower.org/4878oc-iran-threatens-death-to-israel-at-military-parade/.

15. Joel C. Rosenberg, "Why Iran's Top Leaders Believe That the End of Days Has Come," *Fox News*, November 7, 2011, http://www.foxnews.com/opinion/2011/11/07/why-irans-top-leaders-believe-that-end-days-has-come.html.

16. Joel C. Rosenberg, "Understanding Egypt: The Twelfth Imam, and the End of Days," *The Blaze*, February 9, 2011, http://www.theblaze.com/news/2011/02/09/understanding-egypt-the-twelfth-iman-and-the-end-of-days/.

17. Rosenberg, "Iran's Top Leaders."

18. Ben Hubbard, "Dialogue with Iran Is Impossible, Saudi Arabia's Defense Minister Says," *New York Times*, May 2, 2017, https://www.nytimes.com/2017/05/02/world/middleeast/saudi-arabia-iran-defense-minister.html.

19. Ariel Ben Solomon, "Erdogan's Regime Becoming More Dictatorship Than Democracy," *Jerusalem Post*, December 17, 2014, http://www.jpost.com/Middle-East/Analysis-Erdogans-regime-becoming-more-dictatorship-than-democracy-384895.

20. Patrick Kingsley, "Erdogan Claims Vast Powers in Turkey after Narrow Victory in Referendum," *New York Times*, April 16, 2017, https://www.nytimes.com/2017/04/16/world/europe/turkey-referendum-polls-erdogan.html.

21. Eldad Beck, "Erdoğan: 'Liberate Jerusalem' from the Jews," *Ynetnews*, January 6, 2015, http://www.ynetnews.com/articles/0,7340,L-4663579,00.html.

22. Ibid.

23. Burak Bekdil, "Turkey's 'Jerusalem Fetish,'" *Middle East Forum*, May 30, 2015, http://www.meforum.org/5279/turkey-jerusalem-fetish.

24. "Turkey's President Rips into Israel, Tells Muslims to Swarm Temple Mount," *World Israel News*, May 8, 2017, https://worldisraelnews.com /erdogan-rips-into-israel-warns-trump-against-embassy-move/.

25. Amir Tsarfati, "Erdogan Calls on Muslims to 'Join Forces to Protect Jerusalem from Israel's Judaization Attempts,'" *Kehila News Israel*, May 10, 2017, http://kehilanews.com/2017/05/10/erdogan-calls-on-muslims-to -join-forces-to-protect-jerusalem-from-israels-judaization-attempts/.

26. Charles C. Ryrie, *The Best Is Yet to Come* (Chicago: Moody, 1981), 61.

CHAPTER 6: VLADIMIR PUTIN, RISING CZAR

1. Garry Kasparov with Mig Greengard, *Winter Is Coming: Why Vladimir Putin and the Enemies of the Free World Must Be Stopped* (New York: Public Affairs, 2015), xi.

2. David M. Ewalt, "The World's Most Powerful People 2016," *Forbes*, December 14, 2016, http://www.forbes.com/sites/davidewalt/2016/12/14/ the-worlds-most-powerful-people-2016/#2ba85d7e368d.

3. Andrew Marszal, "Vladimir Putin Named Russia's 'Man of the Year'— for the 15th Time in a Row," *Telegraph*, December 17, 2014, http:// www.telegraph.co.uk/news/worldnews/vladimir-putin/11298571 /Vladimir-Putin-named-Russias-Man-of-the-Year-for-the-15th-time-in -a-row.html.

4. Fareed Zakaria, "Why Putin Is World's Most Powerful Man," *CNN*, March 14, 2017, http://www.cnn.com/2017/03/13/opinions/putin-most -powerful-man-world-zakaria/index.html.

5. Marszal, "Vladimir Putin Named Russia's 'Man of the Year.'"

6. Steven Lee Myers, *The New Tsar: The Rise and Reign of Vladimir Putin* (New York: Vintage Books, 2015), 290–91.

7. Ibid. See also Masha Gessen, *The Man without a Face: The Unlikely Rise of Vladimir Putin* (New York: Riverhead Books, 2012), 229.

8. Kasparov, *Winter Is Coming*, 245.

9. Douglas E. Schoen with Evan Roth Smith, *Putin's Master Plan: To Destroy Europe, Divide NATO, and Restore Russian Power and Global Influence* (New York: Encounter Books, 2016), 43.

10. Evan Osnos, David Remnick, and Joshua Yaffa, "Trump, Putin, and the

New Cold War," *New Yorker*, March 6, 2017, http://www.newyorker.com
/magazine/2017/03/06/trump-putin-and-the-new-cold-war.

11. Schoen, *Putin's Master Plan*, 34, 45.

12. Ibid., 34, 46.

13. Ibid., 45.

14. Ibid., 47.

15. Gessen, *Man without a Face*, 229.

16. Osnos, Remnick, and Yaffa, "Trump, Putin, and the New Cold War."

17. Zakaria, "Why Putin Is World's Most Powerful Man."

18. Associated Press, "Putin: Soviet Collapse a 'Genuine Tragedy,'" NBC
    News, April 25, 2005, http://www.nbcnews.com/id/7632057/ns/world
    _news/t/putin-soviet-collapse-genuine-tragedy/#.WRyOF2jys2w.

19. Areg Galstyan, "Is the Eurasian Economic Union Slowly Coming Apart?"
    National Interest, March 29, 2017, http://nationalinterest.org/feature
    /the-eurasian-economic-union-slowing-coming-apart-19947.

20. Emily Tillett, "Condoleezza Rice: Vladimir Putin Trying to Re-establish
    'Russian Greatness,'" *CBS News*, May 7, 2017, http://www.cbsnews.com
    /news/condoleezza-rice-vladimir-putin-trying-to-re-establish-russian
    -greatness/.

21. For a more complete list of key dates, see "Vladimir Putin Fast Facts,"
    CNN Library, February 6, 2017, http://www.cnn.com/2013/01/03/world
    /europe/vladimir-putin---fast-facts/.

22. For an excellent examination of Putin's business dealings, see Myers, *The
    New Tsar*, 281–303.

23. Rob Wile, "Is Vladimir Putin Secretly the Richest Man in the World?"
    Time, January 23, 2017, http://time.com/money/4641093/vladimir-putin
    -net-worth/. See also Emma Burrows, "Vladimir Putin's Inner Circle:
    Who's Who, and How Are They Connected?" *CNN*, March 28, 2017,
    http://www.cnn.com/2017/03/28/europe/vladimir-putins-inner-circle
    /index.html.

24. Schoen, *Putin's Master Plan*, vi.

25. Ibid.

26. Ibid., 13.

27. Ibid., 71.

28. Massimo Calabressi, "Inside Russia's Social Media War on America," *Time*,
    May 18, 2017, http://time.com/4783932/inside-russia-social-media
    -war-america/.

29. Joel C. Rosenberg, "Putin Rising: But Is He 'Gog'?" Joel C. Rosenberg's Blog, August 17, 2011, https://flashtrafficblog.wordpress.com/2011/08/17 /putin-rising-but-is-he-gog/.

CHAPTER 7: RED DAWN RISING: THE WAR OF GOG AND MAGOG

1. David Jeremiah, *Is This the End? Signs of God's Providence in a Disturbing New World* (Nashville: W Publishing Group, 2016), 211.
2. Randall Price, *The Temple and Bible Prophecy: A Definitive Look at Its Past, Present, and Future* (Eugene, OR: Harvest House, 2005), 459.
3. Ibid., 457.
4. Thomas Ice, "Ezekiel 38 & 39 (part 6)," Pre-Trib Research Center, accessed June 10, 2017, http://www.pre-trib.org/articles/view /ezekiel-38-39-part-6.
5. Charles H. Dyer, "Ezekiel," in *The Bible Knowledge Commentary*, ed. John F. Walvoord and Roy B. Zuck (Wheaton, IL: Victor Books, 1985), 1301.
6. Ibid.
7. Walter C. Kaiser Jr., *Preaching and Teaching the Last Things: Old Testament Eschatology for the Life of the Church* (Grand Rapids, MI: Baker Academic, 2011), 89–90.
8. Ibid., 94.
9. See Arnold G. Fruchtenbaum, *The Footsteps of the Messiah: A Study of the Sequence of Prophetic Events*, rev. ed. (Tustin, CA: Ariel Ministries, 2003), 115.
10. Dyer, "Ezekiel," 1301.
11. Fruchtenbaum, *Footsteps of the Messiah*, 115.
12. Randall Price, *Unholy War* (Eugene, OR: Harvest House, 2001), 310.
13. Dyer, "Ezekiel," 1302.
14. Kaiser, *Preaching and Teaching the Last Things*, 97.

CHAPTER 8: HOW CLOSE ARE WE?

1. John F. Walvoord, *The Nations in Prophecy* (Grand Rapids, MI: Zondervan, 1967), 116. Charles Dyer also believes "a reversion to more primitive methods of warfare might be possible." Charles H. Dyer, "Ezekiel," in *The Bible Knowledge Commentary*, ed. John F. Walvoord and Roy B. Zuck (Wheaton, IL: Victor Books, 1985), 1302.
2. Paul P. Enns, ed., *Shepherd's Notes: Ezekiel* (Nashville: B&H, 1998), 92. See

also Charles Lee Feinberg, *The Prophecy of Ezekiel: The Glory of the Lord* (Eugene, OR: Wipf and Stock, 2003), 221.

3. Walter C. Kaiser Jr., *Preaching and Teaching the Last Things: Old Testament Eschatology for the Life of the Church* (Grand Rapids, MI: Baker Academic, 2011), 93.

4. Preterists, who view most biblical prophecy as already fulfilled, hold that the events in Ezekiel 38–39 have already occurred. Gary DeMar, a partial preterist, believes Ezekiel 38–39 was fulfilled in Esther 9. Citing various parallels between the battles in Ezekiel 38–39 and Esther, he claims the two events are "unmistakable" in their similarities. Gary DeMar, *End Times Fiction: A Biblical Consideration of the* Left Behind *Theology* (Nashville: Thomas Nelson, 2001), 12–14. A side-by-side comparison of the two passages, however, reveals substantial inconsistencies, demonstrating that they cannot be describing the same event. But more than this, if Ezekiel 38–39 was fulfilled in the events of Esther 9, why does the book of Esther make no mention of the fulfillment of this prophecy? The omission is telling. Moreover, the Jewish feast of Purim developed out of the Esther event according to Esther 9:20-32. The celebration at Purim includes the public reading of the book of Esther. If Esther 9 were a fulfillment of Ezekiel 38–39, one would expect the Jewish tradition to make some mention of this, yet there is nothing.

5. Walvoord, *Nations in Prophecy*, 105.

6. Randall Price, *The Temple and Bible Prophecy: A Definitive Look at Its Past, Present, and Future* (Eugene, OR: Harvest House, 1999), 458–59.

7. F. F. Bruce, "Eschatology: Understanding the End of Days," *Bible Review* 5 (December 1989): 43.

8. Harold Hoehner maintains that Ezekiel 38–39 will be fulfilled in two phases. Ezekiel 38 (phase 1) will be fulfilled early in the Tribulation, while Ezekiel 39 (phase 2) will be fulfilled at the end of the Tribulation. (Dr. Hoehner presented this view in a PhD seminar I attended.) Likewise, Ralph Alexander sees a double fulfillment with Ezekiel 38 and 39 fulfilled in Revelation 19:17-21 and Revelation 20:8. "The former, in one sense, prefigures the latter." Ralph H. Alexander, *Ezekiel*, Everyman's Bible Commentary (Chicago: Moody, 1976), 128. Charles Ryrie says, "Perhaps the first thrust will begin just before the middle of the Tribulation, with successive waves of the invasion continuing throughout the last part of that

period and building up to Armageddon." Charles C. Ryrie, *The Ryrie Study Bible* (Chicago: Moody, 1995), 1323.

9. Ron Rhodes provides an excellent, evenhanded presentation and evaluation of each of these views in *Northern Storm Rising* (Eugene, OR: Harvest House, 2008), 179–95.

10. John Phillips, *Exploring the Future: A Comprehensive Guide to Bible Prophecy*, 3rd ed. (Grand Rapids, MI: Kregel, 2003), 343.

11. Mike Opelka, "John Kerry: Israel's 'Prosperity' May Be Blocking Peace Process with Palestinians," *The Blaze*, May 28, 2013, http://www.theblaze.com/news/2013/05/28/john-kerry-israels-prosperity-may-be-blocking-peace-process-with-palestinians/.

12. Charles Dyer gives several reasons why identifying Ezekiel 38 with Revelation 20:8 is flawed. He asks, "Why would the people remain on earth after the battle to burn the weapons of war for seven years (Ezek. 38:9-10) instead of entering immediately into eternity?" This kind of dissimilarity between these two passages precludes placing the war of Ezekiel 38–39 at the end of the Millennium. Dyer, "Ezekiel," 1300.

13. Kaiser, *Preaching and Teaching*, 76.

14. Price, *The Temple and Bible Prophecy*, 454.

15. Joel C. Rosenberg, *Epicenter: Why the Current Rumblings in the Middle East Will Change Your Future*, rev. ed. (Carol Stream, IL: Tyndale, 2008), 79.

16. Ibid., 80.

17. David Jeremiah, *Is This the End? Signs of God's Providence in a Disturbing New World* (Nashville: W Publishing Group, 2016), 225–26.

18. Another point against locating this invasion before the Tribulation is that Ezekiel places it in the "last days" or "latter years" of the Jewish people (see Ezekiel 38:8,16). I don't believe the time period before the Tribulation qualifies as Israel's last days. The "last days" or "latter years" for Israel seem to begin with the Tribulation and continue on into the messianic kingdom; therefore, placing this invasion before the Tribulation is not the strongest view. Also, the languge in Ezekiel 38:18-19 of God's fury, wrath, zeal, and anger being poured out on Gog and his armies fits a Tribulation setting for the events of Ezekiel 38 much better than a time period before its onset.

19. Charles Dyer and Mark Tobey, *Clash of Kingdoms: What the Bible Says about Russia, ISIS, Iran, and the End Times* (Nashville: Nelson Books, 2017), 68.

20. The main objection to placing the Battle of Gog and Magog during the

first half of the Tribulation or near its midpoint is Ezekiel 39:9, which says that in the wake of the battle the inhabitants of Israel will make fires with the weapons for a period of seven years. This would mean that if this invasion occurs during the first half of the Tribulation, the weapons would be burned throughout the last half of the Tribulation and even on into the first years of the Millennium. While this is admittedly a problem for the view, it is not fatal. As long as some Jews continue to burn the weapons during the final half of the Tribulation, and briefly into the first three and a half years of the Millennium, the requirements of Ezekiel 39:9 can be fulfilled. John Whitcomb offers a solution to this objection: "I would suggest that this activity of massive cleansing takes place immediately after the second coming of Christ, just after the additional devastation in the holy land called Armageddon. By then, the bodies of Gog's soldiers are nothing but bones (v. 15)." John C. Whitcomb, "Gog from Magog: A Study in Prophetic Chronology," Whitcomb Ministries, 2010, http://media .sermonaudio.com/mediapdf/121110111401.pdf.

21. John Phillips, *Exploring the Future*, 347–48.

22. Jeremiah, *Is This the End?*, 226.

23. John F. Walvoord with Mark Hitchcock, *Armageddon, Oil, and Terror: What the Bible Says about the Future*, rev. ed. (Carol Stream, IL: Tyndale, 2007), 207.

CHAPTER 9: WHAT DOES THE FUTURE HOLD?

1. David Jeremiah, *Is This the End? Signs of God's Providence in a Disturbing New World* (Nashville: W Publishing Group, 2016), 210.

2. Charles Dyer and Mark Tobey, *Clash of Kingdoms: What the Bible Says about Russia, ISIS, Iran, and the End Times* (Nashville: Nelson Books, 2017), 20.

3. Joel C. Rosenberg, *Epicenter: Why the Current Rumblings in the Middle East Will Change Your Future*, rev. ed. (Carol Stream, IL: Tyndale, 2008), 285.

4. J. Vernon McGee, *How Russia Will Be Destroyed* (Pasadena, CA: Thru the Bible Radio Network, n. d.), 10–11, http://www.ttb.org/docs/default -source/Booklets/how-russia-will-be-destroyed.pdf.

5. This list is adapted from a book I coauthored. John F. Walvoord with Mark Hitchcock, *Armageddon, Oil, and Terror: What the Bible Says about the Future*, rev. ed. (Carol Stream, IL: Tyndale, 2007), 203–4.

6. A. W. Tozer, *Preparing for Jesus' Return*, comp. and ed. James L. Snyder (Ventura, CA: Regal, 2012), 21, 191.

7. Ed Hindson, *Final Signs: Amazing Prophecies of the End Times* (Eugene, OR: Harvest House, 1996), 196.

CHAPTER 10: IT'S ALWAYS SOON

1. C. S. Lewis, *The Voyage of the* Dawn Treader (New York: Harper Trophy, 2000), 162.

2. Warren Wiersbe, *Be Ready: Living in Light of Christ's Return, 1 & 2 Thessalonians* (Wheaton, IL: Victor Books, 1979), 137, quoted on Bible.org, accessed June 12, 2017, https://bible.org/seriespage/4-correction -concerning-day-lord-part-1-2-thes-21-5.

3. A. W. Tozer, *Preparing for Jesus' Return*, comp. and ed. James L. Snyder (Ventura, CA: Regal, 2012), 15.

4. Paul N. Benware, *Understanding End Times Prophecy: A Comprehensive Approach*, rev. ed. (Chicago: Moody, 2006), 16.

5. Edward K. Rowell, ed., *Fresh Illustrations for Preaching and Teaching* (Grand Rapids, MI: Baker Books, 1997), 64.

6. Charles Spurgeon, "Watch for Christ's Coming" (sermon #2302), https:// www.ccel.org/ccel/spurgeon/sermons39.xiv.html.

7. Ibid.

8. J. Dwight Pentecost, *Prophecy for Today: God's Purpose and Plan for Our Future*, rev. ed. (Grand Rapids, MI: Discovery House, 1989), 22.

9. David Jeremiah, *Is This the End? Signs of God's Providence in a Disturbing New World* (Nashville: W Publishing Group, 2016), 265.

APPENDIX 2: THE KING OF THE NORTH: THE NORTHERN CONFEDERACY

1. John Walvoord's original chapter on the king of the north goes on to describe "The Emergence of a World Religion," but it does not pertain to the subject of this book, so I've ended the chapter here.

APPENDIX 3: COMMON QUESTIONS RELATED TO RUSSIA, THE MIDDLE EAST, AND THE END OF DAYS

1. Arnold G. Fruchtenbaum, *The Footsteps of the Messiah: A Study of the Sequence of Prophetic Events*, rev. ed. (Tustin, CA: Ariel Ministries, 2003), 111.

2. Ibid., 112.

3. Max Abrahms, Denis Sullivan, and Charles Simpson, "Five Myths about

Syrian Refugees," *Foreign Affairs*, March 22, 2017, https://www
.foreignaffairs.com/articles/europe/2017-03-22/five-myths-about
-syrian-refugees.

4. "ISIS Fast Facts," CNN Library, April 17, 2017, http://edition.cnn
.com/2014/08/08/world/isis-fast-facts/.

5. The main points I've used are taken from Robert Harvey and Philip H.
Towner, *2 Peter and Jude*, The IVP New Testament Commentary Series,
ed. Grant R. Osborne (Downers Grove, IL: IVP Academic, 2009),
118–19.

6. Ibid., 118.

7. Ibid.

8. D. Edmond Hiebert, *Second Peter and Jude: An Expositional Commentary*
(Greenville, SC: BJU Press, 1989) 153.

9. Harvey and Towner, *2 Peter and Jude*, 119.

10. Ibid.

11. Michael Green, *The Second Epistle General of Peter and the General Epistle
of Jude*, The Tyndale New Testament Commentaries, gen. ed. Leon Morris,
rev. ed. (Grand Rapids, MI: Eerdmans, 1989), 148.

About the Author

Mark Hitchcock was born and raised in Oklahoma City, Oklahoma. He attended Oklahoma State University and graduated from law school in 1984. After working for a judge at the Oklahoma Court of Criminal Appeals for four years, Mark was led to attend Dallas Theological Seminary, graduating in 1991. Since that time, he has served as senior pastor of Faith Bible Church in Edmond, Oklahoma. He completed his PhD at Dallas Theological Seminary in 2005 and serves as an associate professor of Bible exposition at DTS. He has authored more than thirty books related to end-times Bible prophecy that have sold more than one million copies. His books have been translated into more than ten languages. Mark is a frequent speaker at churches and prophecy conferences both in the United States and internationally. Mark and his wife, Cheryl, live in Edmond, Oklahoma. They have two sons, Justin (married to Natalee) and Samuel, and two grandchildren.